Carla's Comfort Foods

Carla's Comfort Foods

Favorite Dishes from Around the World

Carla Hall

with Genevieve Ko

Photography by Frances Janisch
Design by Jennifer Barry

ATRIA BOOKS

NEW YORK   LONDON   TORONTO   SYDNEY   NEW DELHI

B O O K S

A Division of Simon & Schuster, Inc.
1230 Avenue of the Americas
New York, NY 10020

First Atria Books hardcover edition April 2014

ATRIA B O O K S and colophon are trademarks of Simon & Schuster, Inc.

For information about special discounts for bulk purchases, please contact Simon & Schuster
Special Sales at 1-866-506-1949 or business@simonandschuster.com.

The Simon & Schuster Speakers Bureau can bring authors to your live event. For more
information or to book an event, contact the Simon & Schuster Speakers Bureau at
1-866-248-3049 or visit our website at www.simonspeakers.com.

Designed and produced by Jennifer Barry Design, Fairfax, California
Jacket photography by Frances Janisch
Interior photography by Frances Janisch, except for photographs on
page 40 by Jennifer Barry and on page 93 by Carla Hall

Manufactured in the United States of America

10 9 8 7 6 5 4 3 2

Library of Congress Cataloging in Publication Data
Hall, Carla.
    Carla's Comfort Food : favorite dishes from around the world / Carla Hall and Genevieve Ko ;
design by Jennifer Barry ; photography by Frances Janisch.
        pages cm; Includes index.
1. International cooking. 2. Comfort food.   I. Ko, Genevieve. II. Title.
    TX725.A1H26 2014
    641.59—dc23
    2013035094

ISBN 978-1-4516-6222-1
ISBN 978-1-4516-6224-5 (ebook)

Contents

Vegetarian Entrées

*H*ere's what's so great about being on the daily television food-talk show *The Chew* in the age of social media: I actually get to know my viewers! That's what I love most about food—connecting with people through shared meals and recipes. I'm all about comfort food made easy and accessible. And I'm all about lovin' people: the people my food is inspired by and the people I'm creating the recipes for. I've brought those two passions together here with simple, soulful recipes, drawn from flavors and friends around the globe.

The warming dishes in here highlight international flavors, but my recipes are for American home cooks. No technique is too complicated and no ingredient too hard to find. I've removed all the kitchen barriers that make cooking other cuisines challenging, and, in the process, I hope I've taken down those barriers that we put up when we're confronted with something or someone different. I've tried to do it the best way I know how: good food! I'm gonna take you from Nashville to Naples to Nigeria so you can taste and see how we're all united by great meals shared with family and friends.

You know how else we're connected? Through fundamental cooking techniques. Over decades as a chef, I've come to realize that there are a limited number of ways to prepare food. There's only so much we can do to get a chicken from raw to cooked. But the seasonings we add in the process can change in a million ways! So I've taken staple ingredients and basic dishes and spun them into variations from different countries. If you're bored of the same ol' chicken soup, I've got delicious new ones for you. No highfalutin tricks to them! I've simply swapped spices and seasonings in the same superfast and easy stovetop technique, so you get totally fresh flavors without extra effort. I've done that throughout the book, starting with comforting American and Southern staples, then going from there. You love creamy cod chowder? I got that. Then I'll show you how to do a coconut Latin fish stew and a spicy tomato African one and a tangy Asian one. Just those little changes in the recipes and OMG! You'll taste the dishes and think, "I'm going to all these new places!"

This is the sort of cooking I've been doing my whole career. I master a technique, then I think about global spices and seasonings and try using them in different ways.

I follow threads of flavor through cultures and ultimately put together a dish that's easily accessible in taste and execution. And that's what you'll get in these pages!

Even before you get to the recipes, you'll see my overview of some of the world's major cuisines with an international spice chart and pantry that shows what unifies a particular cuisine and ties it to foods from other regions. You can use it to create your own international dishes and see how easy it is. All it takes are a few different supermarket ingredients: a little bit of spice, flavorful veggies and herbs, and easy-to-find sauces. I'm takin' y'all on a spice journey!

There is, of course, no way I could cover all of the world's cuisines and dishes in the recipes, even if I used *all* of the seasonings in my spice chart. I've collected the most comforting, homey meals that I love from other cultures and put my own spin on them. Stayin' true to the spirit of the dishes, I've tweaked them to my taste. I imagine that's what grandmas have been doing for generations. You'll get my Arroz con Pollo in here and find a zillion others all around the globe. I'm not claiming to have the ultimate or definitive versions of anything here, just my own super tasty and satisfying takes that are quick and easy to make in any American kitchen.

One of the greatest things about my international twists on simple techniques is how it'll help us all eat healthier. That's why this book starts with easy-to-find veggies and does 'em in soups, salads, side dishes, preserves, and main dishes. With my globally seasoned dishes, you'll get an all-new taste of the same ol' same ol' produce

and build meals with veggies as the stars. The fish, poultry, and meat dishes that follow are yummy, too, and will liven up your daily meals again. And don't worry—I didn't forget about dessert. (I never do!) I've stayed a little closer to home with my sweets, and have fun new treats for you to try.

In the process of creating dishes for this book, I had an epiphany. I was chatting with my *Chew* co-host Daphne Oz, and we both realized that it's so easy to forget our culinary heritage when we set down roots in cities so different from our families' hometowns. Her family hails from Turkey and mine from the South. (Yes, it is a different culture from New York City!) We bonded over the importance of preserving our families' dishes for future generations. I've done that in this book for my family, and I hope I've done that for other families who are a bit farther removed from their origins and may not have old recipes written down. If your family who came from Greece generations ago wants to take a crack at spanakopita or baklava for the first time, I've got that here!

Part of the fun of preserving recipes is putting our own fingerprints on them. I've included lots of ways to change these dishes to your taste. For you hotheads out there, I've told you how to dial up the chiles. (If you don't like heat, just leave them out!) The important thing about trying new dishes from other cultures—or even our own—is to remember that you may just need to adjust something to make it taste the way you like it. That's what I did in this book. I've adjusted dishes to suit my style— lots of deep flavor, complex textures, and all-around yummy-ness. Sometimes that meant abandoning traditional techniques, even ones my family taught me. For example, Grandma Thelma always, always floured her chicken skin before frying it for smothered chicken in milk gravy. Well, I think that makes the skin flabby. So I crisped the skin naked and added the flour to thicken the gravy later. I think Grandma Thelma

would just be happy to know that I'm still making that dish and teaching it to her great-grandchildren, too.

That's sayin' a lot because my family's the reason this book even exists. Whenever I talk about my love of food, I always emphasize how it all started with my love of our Sunday suppers. That's how we all relate to food, right? It's those relationships that make comfort food comforting and that make certain meals stand out in our memories. This is a cookbook of collective food memories that reflect my intuitive cooking style of connecting with people. I don't have a technical term for what I do: I just listen to my friends, family, and fans, chat with them, and then create a dish based on my sixth sense for what would make everyone happy.

I value people and how people live and cook before I value being a chef, so my approach to the dishes in this cookbook is very homey. I want to inspire you to cook, try different foods, and just explore new cuisines. I do this everywhere I go and I can assure you it makes for good cooking . . . and it's a great way to make new friends. Any time, any place, I will start talking to people and asking them about their stories. My way into the conversation is always food. It's what I do, how I think. What I've realized over the years, getting to know so many people around the country, is that food can bring us together. I often think that if people could just share a meal together, the discord between different groups might be lessened. It's not so easy to hate people with whom you're sharing good food.

We're all connected through food, and the dishes in this book show that we're more alike than different. Sure, I grew up with grits, but it's served as polenta in Italy. Something as simple as a great dish shows how we're all really very similar. I love seeing—and tasting—how home-cooked food works in uniting people, and I hope you will, too.

Carla

International Spice Chart

A smart place to start cooking globally is by stocking up on what you need for each cuisine. The lists below are by no means exhaustive, but they're a great place to get a hang of the basics. They're also a way to see which flavors go together if you want to try experimenting more with any one type of cuisine.

Aromatics	Herbs	Spices	Misc.
American onions chiles lemon scallions *(green onions)*	dill thyme mint allspice parsley bay leaves	cayenne mustard cinnamon nutmeg cumin paprika	butter ketchup cream white vinegar sour cream
Southern onions garlic chiles lemon	dill thyme mint bay leaves parsley	cayenne mustard cinnamon nutmeg cumin paprika curry turmeric celery seeds	butter hot sauce cream sour cream cider vinegar
British/Irish onions scallions *(green onions)*	parsley thyme	cinnamon curry mustard nutmeg	butter cream Worcestershire
Hungarian onions	dill parsley	bay leaves paprika cinnamon caraway seeds mustard	butter cream sour cream Worcestershire
German onions	parsley	cinnamon mustard nutmeg	butter cream
French onions leeks garlic lemon shallots	dill parsley tarragon thyme	bay leaves cinnamon mustard nutmeg	butter cream wine vinegar olive oil
Italian onions garlic chiles lemon	basil oregano parsley rosemary	cinnamon	butter wine cream vinegar olive oil balsamic olives vinegar capers parmesan
Spanish onions lemon garlic lime chiles scallions *(green onions)*	parsley bay leaves cayenne	cinnamon paprika saffron olive oil	sherry sherry vinegar olives

Aromatics		Herbs	Spices		Misc.
Greek					
onions	ginger	mint	bay leaves	coriander	olive oil
garlic	lemon	oregano	cayenne	cumin	olives
shallots	lime	parsley	cinnamon	nutmeg	yogurt
scallions *(green onions)*					
Persian					
		cilantro	bay leaves	cumin	olive oil
onions	lemon	mint	cayenne	saffron	sesame seeds
garlic	lime	parsley	cinnamon	sumac	yogurt
ginger			coriander		
Middle Eastern					
		cilantro	bay leaves	coriander	olive oil
onions	lemon	mint	cayenne	cumin	
garlic	lime	parsley	cinnamon	turmeric	
chiles					
Indian/South Asian					
			cardamom	cumin	
onions	chiles	cilantro	cayenne	curry	coconut
garlic	lime	mint	cinnamon	mustard	
ginger			coriander	turmeric	
			garam masala		
Moroccan					
onions		cilantro	cardamom	curry	olive oil
garlic		mint	cayenne	nutmeg	preserved lemon
chiles		parsley	cinnamon	paprika	green olives
lime			coriander	turmeric	
			cumin		
African					
onions	chiles		cayenne	cumin	coconut
garlic	lime	cilantro	cinnamon	curry	
scallions *(green onions)*					
green bell peppers					
Caribbean/Bahamian					
		cilantro	allspice	cumin	coconut
onions	chiles	oregano	cayenne	curry	
garlic	lime	thyme	celery seeds		
green bell peppers			cinnamon		
Latin/Mexican					
		cilantro	bay leaves	cumin	crema
onions	chiles	oregano	cayenne	epazote	queso
garlic	lime		cinnamon	turmeric	
scallions *(green onions)*			coriander		
East Asian					
onions	chiles	basil	cinnamon		soy sauce sesame oil
garlic	lime	cilantro	curry		rice wine rice vinegar
ginger					oyster sauce
scallions *(green onions)*					hoisin sauce
Southeast Asian					
onions	ginger lime	mint	cinnamon		soy sauce
garlic	chiles	basil	curry		fish sauce
shallots	lemongrass	cilantro			coconut milk
scallions *(green onions)*					rice vinegar

Soups & Salads

Here in America, we tend to start a meal with soup or salad. In other areas of the world, these staples are served as part of the main spread, alone as the main course, or at the end. I love the way switching up when and how a course is served can give us a new perspective on food.

The dishes in this chapter are super simple and are meant to be tweaked to taste. For the slaws, be sure to season with salt, and add more acid for a tart bite or more oil to mellow it out. Throw in more of your favorite veg or leave out the ones you really don't like. With the soups, keep tasting and seasoning as you cook, and feel free to thin with more broth at the end if you prefer a lighter consistency. Salads and soups are the best place to start toying around, making these dishes your own—and to get into the habit of tasting your food as you prepare it.

Tomato Soups

Whenever I make a tomato dish, I always have a little chuckle. I hated tomatoes as a kid. While my sister, Kim, ate them like apples, I wouldn't even touch them. I especially didn't like tomato soup because I found it so acidic. As an adult who's since totally fallen for tomatoes, I've offered two different soups here—cold and crisp and hot and stewy— to show how versatile they are. All you need to make these great is ripe tomatoes, preferably heirloom ones that have complex flavors. Don't worry if they're ugly and lumpy. What matters is how tasty they are on the inside . . .

There's this window deep in summer when tomatoes seem to be literally spilling out of markets. They're so fat and juicy! I bring home bags and bags of them, and soup is one of my favorite ways to get the most out of their seasonal sweetness.

SPANISH

Tomato-Water Gazpacho

Serves 6

The first time I'd ever heard of gazpacho was while watching the movie Women on the Verge of a Nervous Breakdown. *The character makes a chunky batch in a blender and spikes it with sleeping pills. When I got around to creating my own version, I decided to make it super smooth instead. In fact, the soup itself is well-seasoned tomato water and the vegetables go on top as a garnish. It's an elegant way of serving a traditionally rustic soup and great for making ahead since it strains overnight.*

Soup

4 large beefsteak tomatoes, cored and cut into quarters

$1/2$ serrano chile, chopped

$1/4$ red onion, chopped

1 garlic clove

$1/2$ fennel bulb, chopped

1 celery rib, chopped

$1/2$ red bell pepper, stemmed, seeded, and chopped

$1/2$ teaspoon kosher salt

$1/4$ teaspoon sugar

Garnish

$1/4$ seedless cucumber, peeled and finely diced

1 plum tomato, peeled, seeded, and finely diced

1 teaspoon grated fresh horseradish or drained prepared horseradish

1 teaspoon finely chopped fresh cilantro leaves

2 teaspoons thinly sliced scallions (green onions)

Kosher salt and freshly ground black pepper

1 lime

2 tablespoons sherry vinegar

Juice of $1/2$ lemon

1 To make the soup: In a food processor or blender, combine all of the ingredients. Puree until smooth. Line a fine-mesh sieve with cheesecloth and set it over a large nonreactive bowl. Pour the puree into the cheesecloth, cover, and refrigerate overnight.

2 When ready to serve, gather the cheesecloth around the solids and gently squeeze out any last bits of liquid into the sieve. Discard the solids.

3 To make the garnish: In a medium bowl, toss together the cucumber, tomato, horseradish, cilantro, scallion, and a pinch each of salt and pepper. Zest the lime into the mixture, then squeeze in the juice of half of the lime. Taste and adjust the seasonings.

4 Stir the sherry vinegar, lemon juice, and the juice from the remaining lime half into the tomato water. Taste and adjust the seasonings. Divide among soup bowls and add the garnish. Serve cold.

Carla's Tips

• The flavors in this soup are so clear and purely veg that you need to keep tasting to season it properly. The amounts in the recipe are just suggestions based on the ripe summer produce I use when making this soup. Add more lemon, lime, vinegar, salt, sugar, and/or pepper to get it just the way you like it.

• If you're going to be serving this on a really hot day and you want to set it out early, freeze half of the tomato water in ice cube trays. Combine the ice cubes with the chilled tomato water in serving dishes, and add the garnish. By the time guests sit down to eat, the soup will still be cold.

Tomato-Corn Chowder

Serves 6

This soup marks the beginning of my cooking career. At my first restaurant job, chef Jon Dornbusch had me make this chowder, a staple on his menu at the Henley Park Hotel. I hadn't worked with Mexican flavors and had no clue how to handle the huge 5-quart blender. Thankfully, it all came together beautifully. I was fascinated by the addition of cumin and the deep orange color of the finished soup. In my mind's eye, corn chowder should be yellow, but this is tinted by the tomatoes and chiles. I've adjusted my perception of what corn soup should look like and am glad I have!

2 tablespoons canola oil

2 large yellow onions, diced

Kosher salt

4 garlic cloves, chopped

1 teaspoon ground cumin

1 teaspoon dried epazote or oregano

1 teaspoon ground Mexican chile, such as ancho

1 small yuca or Idaho potato, peeled and finely diced (see Carla's Tips)

4 cups Vegetable Stock (page 103) or store-bought unsalted vegetable broth

4 cups diced tomatoes

5 ears corn, husks and silks removed, kernels cut off and reserved, cobs reserved

Mexican crema or sour cream, for serving

Lime wedges, for serving

Avocado, peeled, pitted, and sliced, for serving

Fresh cilantro leaves, chopped, for serving

1 Heat the oil in a large saucepan over medium heat. Add the onions and ½ teaspoon salt and cook, stirring occasionally, until the onions are translucent, about 5 minutes. Add the garlic and cook, stirring, for 1 minute. Add the cumin, epazote, and chile and cook, stirring, for 1 minute.

2 Add the yuca, stock, tomatoes with their juices, and corn cobs. Bring to a boil, then reduce the heat and simmer until the yuca is tender, about 30 minutes. Add the corn kernels and cook just until heated through and still crisp-tender, about 3 minutes. Discard the corn cobs.

3 Using an immersion blender or stand blender (working in batches if necessary), puree about half of the soup until thickened. It should be creamy but still have bits of vegetables throughout. Stir the puree into the remaining soup. Serve with the crema, lime, avocado, and cilantro.

• •

Carla's Tips

• Yuca's a starchy vegetable that's also known as cassava. It's similar to potatoes but even starchier, with a mild sweetness.

• •

Creamy Soups

I'm a creamy soup kinda gal. They're comforting yet elegant, simple but full of flavor. The coolest thing about creamy soups from other parts of the world is that they don't necessarily contain any cream! In the recipes that follow, vegetables, eggs, and even legumes thicken the liquid naturally while adding complex flavors. For smooth blended soups, you need a good blender or immersion blender. If you want to get refined in the kitchen, you can pass a blended soup through a fine-mesh sieve. That's a nice touch restaurant chefs always incorporate, but it's not at all necessary for a comforting bowl of soup at home.

Vadouvan Curried Carrot Soup

Serves 6

Sure, being a Top Chef contestant meant trying to beat fellow chefs in the kitchen. But it also meant learning a lot from creative, talented cooks, like the time Jamie Lauren shared her vadouvan with me. It's a super intense French-Indian curry mix. You can find it in gourmet shops; the best varieties are freshly made and moist from caramelized onions. You can substitute curry paste or powder in a pinch and still end up with a tasty soup.

2 tablespoons extra virgin olive oil

2 pounds carrots, peeled and sliced

1 large yellow onion, chopped

1 leek (white and pale green parts only), trimmed, diced, and thoroughly rinsed

1 celery rib, chopped

6 garlic cloves, sliced

Kosher salt and freshly ground black pepper

1 tablespoon vadouvan

4 cups Vegetable Stock (page 103) or store-bought unsalted vegetable broth, plus more if desired

1 tablespoon fresh lemon juice

¼ teaspoon sugar

¼ cup heavy cream

Chile oil (optional)

1 Heat the oil in a large saucepan over medium-low heat. Add the carrots, onion, leek, celery, garlic, and a pinch each of salt and pepper. Cook, stirring occasionally, until the onion is translucent, about 10 minutes.

2 Stir in the vadouvan and cook for 1 minute. Add the stock, lemon juice, and sugar. Bring to a boil, then reduce the heat to a simmer. Cook until the carrots are tender, about 30 minutes.

3 Using an immersion blender or stand blender (working in batches if necessary), puree until silky smooth. Stir in the cream, and add additional stock if you prefer a thinner soup. Season to taste with salt and pepper. Drizzle the chile oil on top, if using, and serve.

• •

Carla's Tips

• **Swap Out:** If you can't find vadouvan, use a good curry powder or paste instead.

• •

Left: Fresh carrots with Vadouvan spice mixture

GREEK

Avgolemono: Egg and Lemon Soup

Serves 6

I'll be honest: The first time I tasted this in a restaurant, I didn't find it very memorable. Shocking, given my love of lemons. Then Michael Symon made an awesome avgolemono on The Chew. *It piqued my interest in this really cool dish. It's super lemony and creamy at the same time, but without any cream. The magic ingredient? Eggs! Very gently heated and stirred simultaneously, they thicken the chicken soup into velvety goodness. What makes my version special is the addition of fresh mint. Traditionally, if the soup comes with any herbs at all, it is flavored with dill. I often pair lemon and mint and found it's extra-tasty here.*

1 tablespoon extra virgin olive oil

1½ cups finely diced yellow onions

¾ cup finely diced celery

¾ cup finely diced carrots

Kosher salt and freshly ground black pepper

6 cups Chicken Stock (page 103) or store-bought unsalted chicken broth

1 cup orzo

3 large eggs, at room temperature

2 tablespoons cornstarch

½ cup fresh lemon juice

Lemon slices, for garnish

1 tablespoon thinly sliced fresh mint leaves

1 Heat the oil in a large saucepan over medium heat. Add the onions, celery, carrots, and a pinch each of salt and pepper. Cook, stirring occasionally, until the onions are soft, about 7 minutes.

2 Stir in 4 cups of the chicken stock and season to taste with salt. Bring to a boil, then stir in the orzo. Cook until just al dente, about 2 minutes less than the package instructions. Reduce the heat to maintain a very low simmer.

3 Meanwhile, bring the remaining 2 cups stock to a boil in a small saucepan. In a medium bowl, whisk the eggs and cornstarch until pale yellow and thick. Continue whisking and add the hot stock, then the lemon juice, in a steady stream.

4 Stir the egg mixture into the orzo soup, but do not let the soup come to a boil! If it does, the soup could curdle. Garnish with lemon slices and mint leaves, and serve immediately.

• •

Carla's Tips

• Chicken stock is traditional here, but you can use Vegetable Stock (page 103) to make this vegetarian.

• •

Caraway Bacon Potato Soup

Serves 6

I've taken vichyssoise, the classic French potato soup, and moved it in a decidedly Hungarian direction with caraway and sour cream. I love having little bits of texture in my smooth soups, and the bite of the caraway seeds works perfectly here. It's heartier this way and super comforting on chilly nights.

3 strips bacon

1 large yellow onion, chopped

1 celery rib, chopped

Kosher salt and freshly ground black pepper

2 garlic cloves, finely chopped

1 fresh or dried bay leaf

1 teaspoon caraway seeds, toasted, plus more for garnish

2 large Idaho potatoes, peeled and chopped (4 cups)

6 cups Vegetable or Chicken Stock (page 103) or store-bought unsalted broth

1/2 cup sour cream

Fresh flat-leaf parsley leaves, chopped, for garnish

1 In a large saucepan, cook the bacon over medium heat, turning occasionally, until browned and crisp, about 8 minutes. Transfer to paper towels to drain. Crumble and reserve.

2 To the fat in the pan, add the onion, celery, and a pinch each of salt and pepper. Cook, stirring occasionally, until the onion is translucent, about 7 minutes. Add the garlic, bay leaf, and caraway seeds. Cook, stirring, until the garlic is golden, about 2 minutes.

3 Add the potatoes, stock, and a generous pinch of salt. Bring to a boil, then reduce the heat to a simmer and cook until the potatoes are very soft, about 25 minutes. Discard the bay leaf.

4 Remove from the heat. Using an immersion blender or stand blender (working in batches if necessary), puree until just smooth. Stir in the sour cream and season to taste with salt and pepper. Divide among serving bowls and garnish with the parsley, crumbled bacon, and caraway seeds.

• •

Carla's Tips

• Pureed soups like this are quick because you don't have to worry about how nicely you dice your vegetables. No one's going to see them! Just make sure they're all the same size so they cook evenly.

• Be sure to stop pureeing as soon as the potatoes are smooth. If you keep going, they'll get gluey.

• •

Red Lentil Soup

Serves 6

When simmered until soft, red lentils break down into total creaminess. Onions add a deep, natural sweetness, spices punch up the flavor, and coconut milk makes the mix even creamier. I love that this soup is vegan and tastes so satisfying.

1 tablespoon canola oil

2 large yellow onions, finely diced

Kosher salt

2 garlic cloves, coarsely chopped

One 1-inch piece fresh ginger, peeled and minced

2 teaspoons ground coriander

2 teaspoons ground cumin

1 teaspoon turmeric

2 cups red or orange lentils, picked over

6 cups Vegetable Stock (page 103) or store-bought unsalted vegetable broth, plus more if desired

Freshly ground black pepper

1/2 cup coconut milk

2 tablespoons chopped fresh cilantro leaves

1 Heat the oil in a large saucepan over medium heat. Add the onions and a pinch of salt and cook, stirring occasionally, until golden brown and tender, about 5 minutes. Add the garlic and ginger and cook, stirring, for 1 minute. Then add the spices and cook, stirring, for 1 minute.

2 Stir in the lentils until well coated, and then stir in the vegetable stock. Bring to a boil, reduce the heat to maintain a steady simmer, and cook, stirring occasionally, until the lentils are very tender and the soup is thick, about 20 minutes. Season to taste with salt and pepper.

3 Stir in the coconut milk, and more stock if you prefer a thinner soup. Garnish with the cilantro.

• •

Carla's Tips

• If you prefer a smoother soup, you can puree this with a blender.

• •

Form Over Function

When I cook a dish, I think about how it will look as much as how it will taste. That's important, sure, but it's gotten me into trouble a few times. Take lentils. When I started cooking in professional kitchens, I was always very careful to not overcook lentils and let them become mushy. French du Puy lentils work wonderfully with this treatment— even when cooked through, their tiny pebble-like shape stays intact.

When I saw a bag of red lentils at the store, I was so excited by their gorgeous sunset orange color. I decided to cook them for a fancy Thanksgiving dinner that my roommate and friend Greta and I decided to host at my house. Of course, I didn't bother to find out how they're best prepared. I figured I'd just cook them the same way I did French lentils to keep their color bright and their shape pretty.

And they were beautiful. I was so happy with my stunning side dish, I didn't bother to taste it until we all sat down to feast. One spoonful of those crunchy bites and I wanted to convince my guests that this was how they were supposed to taste. But Greta took a bite, twisted her lips up, and shouted, "They're un-done-tay!" Yup, that was when she coined the term, and I now use it to describe anything I completely undercook in an attempt to cook them until just tender.

After that night, I scoured cookbooks for red lentil recipes and discovered that they're meant to be cooked until they're so soft that their shape disintegrates to mush and they turn a muddy brown. They're ugly that way, but so delicious. Sometimes, something's gotta give if you want a really tasty dish.

Slaws

Cheap and cheerful: That's one of my cooking mottos and slaw totally fits the bill. A head of cabbage is cheap and goes a long, long way. If you're not into cabbage, you can make a slaw with any crunchy veg cut into thin matchsticks. I've always gotta have the refreshing crunch of raw veggies to balance richer dishes. Be sure to use a sharp knife to slice your cabbage or other vegetables. If you have a mandoline, you can use it for fast, even slicing.

 BAHAMIAN

Creamy Cabbage Slaw

Serves 8

Warning: I love tart! I push everything to the tart edge. Even though this slaw is bound by creamy mayonnaise, I add vinegar to make the dressing tangy. The point is to create a side dish that cuts through main dishes that are meaty or deep-fried or both. That's why Lady Caroline, the woman for whom I cooked as a private chef in the Bahamas, always requested this slaw to go with her special birthday spread of blackened fish, rice 'n' beans, and fried plantains.

8 cups very, very thinly sliced cabbage

1 1/2 teaspoons kosher salt

1/2 cup mayonnaise

1 tablespoon plus 1 teaspoon cider vinegar

1 teaspoon sugar

1/2 teaspoon celery seeds

1/2 cup shredded carrot

1 tablespoon grated yellow onion

1 In a colander, toss the cabbage with the salt. Let sit for 10 minutes, then squeeze dry, wringing the cabbage in paper towels to get out as much moisture as possible.

2 Meanwhile, in a large bowl, whisk together the mayonnaise, vinegar, sugar, and celery seeds. Add the carrot, onion, and cabbage and toss until well coated. You can cover and refrigerate the slaw for up to 1 day; toss it again before serving.

Serve with a pulled pork sandwich or with grilled or fried meat or fish.

. . . .

Carla's Tips

• The salting step is particularly important because it prevents the cabbage's natural juices from running into the dressing and diluting it.

. . . .

Cucumber-Carrot Slaw with Crunchy Noodles

Serves 8

My husband, Matthew, and I love chef Susur Lee's Singapore Slaw at his restaurant Zentan in Washington, D.C. But there's a reason we eat it at the restaurant: It has more ingredients than I can count! When I was craving it at home one night, I decided to make my own streamlined version. It's not quite Susur's masterpiece, but it captures the spirit of the original.

Ginger-Plum Dressing

⅓ cup chopped dried plums

⅓ cup rice vinegar

2 teaspoons finely chopped scallion (green onion) whites

1 teaspoon minced peeled fresh ginger

½ teaspoon kosher salt

⅓ cup canola oil

⅓ cup water

Slaw

Canola oil, for frying

2 ounces rice vermicelli

1 cup julienned seedless cucumber

1 cup julienned carrot

1 cup julienned jicama

½ cup bean sprouts

½ cup thinly sliced scallions (green onions)

2 tablespoons chopped fresh cilantro

2 tablespoons chopped roasted unsalted peanuts, plus more for garnish

1 To make the dressing: In a blender, puree the plums, vinegar, scallions, ginger, and salt until smooth. With the machine running, add the oil, then the water, in a slow, steady stream and puree until emulsified.

2 To make the slaw: Line a large plate with paper towels. Fill a small saucepan with oil to a depth of 1 inch, and heat over medium-high heat until hot (350°F). Break the noodle bundles into 5-inch-long pieces. Add a handful of noodles to the oil. They'll puff and turn white immediately. Cook just until they're all puffed, about 5 seconds. Use a slotted spoon to transfer the noodles to the paper towels. Repeat with the remaining noodles.

3 In a large bowl, toss the cucumber, carrot, jicama, sprouts, scallions, cilantro, peanuts, and ½ cup of the dressing until well mixed. You can add more dressing to taste. Right before serving, top with the noodles and more peanuts. Eat right away! Get some noodles and slaw in each bite, but eat fast because the noodles get soggy.

. . . .

Carla's Tips

• Yes, "dried plums" is just a fancy way of saying prunes. They're delicious no matter what you call them, but maybe a little more appetizing as "plums." Am I right?

. . . .

Tangy Hot Cabbage Slaw

Serves 8

There's a pupusas *joint near my home in Washington, D.C., that gets packed as dinnertime approaches. Their hot griddled cornmeal cakes come with a little plastic container of this slaw, which balances the hearty meat-and-cheese fillings. This super simple slaw is just as good on any other cornmeal creation, from tacos to arepas to Beef and Pepper Enchiladas (page 139) to Black Bean Empanadas (page 166).*

1/2 cup white vinegar

1 teaspoon kosher salt

1/2 teaspoon sugar

1/4 teaspoon freshly ground black pepper

8 cups very thinly sliced cabbage

1/2 cup very thinly sliced red onion

1/2 cup shredded carrot

1 jalapeño chile, stemmed, seeded, and minced

1/2 teaspoon dried oregano

1 In a large bowl, whisk the vinegar, salt, sugar, and pepper until the sugar dissolves.

2 Add the cabbage, onion, carrot, jalapeño, and oregano and toss well. You can cover the slaw and refrigerate it overnight, but it's best fresh.

• •

Carla's Tips

• Adjust the amount of onion to your taste.

• **Some Like It Hot:** Keep the seeds in the chile and add another if you'd like.

• •

Vegetables

My favorite, favorite food: vegetables!

Whenever I travel, I check out the local markets to see what farmers are growing and ask local home cooks how they prepare those veggies. The coolest thing about global food is the huge variety of produce out there. Since I can't always get my hands on what I've tasted abroad, I like to re-create the same flavors with the vegetables available at home. It's amazing how naturally spices and seasonings adapt to similar types of veggies. You'll see familiar vegetables in the pages that follow, but you may be surprised by the flavors I apply to them. I'm talkin' spicy pea chutney, crab in spinach, and coconut-sauced squash.

Trying these new dishes may just be the secret to getting the veggie-haters in your life to transform into veggie-lovers. When I was little, I hated green beans and tomatoes and a long list of greens. Over the years, I came to realize that I didn't hate the vegetables themselves, but the way they were prepared. So you never know—these dishes may just change your mind about what you think you like and don't like.

Though the flavors differ around the world, there are a few key tips and techniques:

- Look for the freshest produce you can find, ideally locally grown without pesticides.
- Rinse and dry well. There's nothing worse than grit in your food!
- To make sure all your vegetables cook at the same rate, cut them the same size.
- Vegetables range in flavor and sweetness, so keep tasting and seasoning as you're cooking, up until the time you serve them.

Peas

By now, anyone who knows me knows I love peas. Fresh off the vine, they have a distinct sweetness and crisp pop that's unlike anything else. When I catered professionally, I never considered serving peas out of season . . . until customers demanded them in the dead of winter. So I tried frozen peas and have relied on them ten months out of the year ever since. They're already cooked, so you simply thaw them before cooking. Definitely use fresh peas if you have them—they're so, so yummy—and when you can't, go for frozen.

How to Cook Frozen Peas

You don't. They're already parcooked for you, so be sure to avoid overcooking them in any dish. You usually add them just at the very end. What you do have to do before adding them to a dish is thaw them. The best way is to let them sit on the counter while you prep the rest of the ingredients. If you don't have time for that, rinse them in a colander under hot water.

How to Cook Fresh Peas

Just boil them. Really. Add the shelled peas to a saucepan of rapidly boiling water and keep tasting them until they're just tender. Peas cook at different rates depending on their variety, freshness, and size, so the only way to tell when they're done is by tasting. They're generally firmer than frozen peas, but should be tender-crisp.

Last Supper Buttered Tarragon Peas

Serves 4

As a contestant on Top Chef, *I had the privilege of making culinary legend Jacques Pépin's ideal last supper. He swooned over these peas! His happy reaction actually brought tears to my eyes. Maybe it was because I would want these peas at my last supper, too. And apparently I'm not the only one. I didn't include this recipe in my first cookbook and I can't tell you how many requests I've gotten for it. So here you go, folks: the peas that'll let you leave this world happy.*

2 tablespoons unsalted butter

¼ cup minced shallots

Kosher salt

2 cups cooked fresh peas or thawed frozen peas

2 teaspoons finely chopped fresh tarragon leaves, plus whole leaves for garnish

½ teaspoon chopped fresh thyme leaves

1 teaspoon freshly grated lemon zest

¼ cup water

1 In a large skillet, melt 1 tablespoon of the butter over medium-low heat. Add the shallots and ¼ teaspoon salt. Cook, stirring, until the shallots are just translucent, about 1 minute. Add the peas, reduce the heat to low, and cook, stirring, until heated through.

2 Add the tarragon, thyme, lemon zest, water, and remaining 1 tablespoon butter. Cook, stirring, until the peas are glazed, about 5 minutes. Garnish with tarragon leaves and serve immediately.

• •

Carla's Tips

• One of my favorite French techniques is combining butter and water to gloss fresh vegetables. Butter makes the sauce creamy and the water keeps it from becoming too rich.

• To get my beloved lemon in here, I add zest to the glaze. Fresh juice would discolor the peas and the zest adds a nice floral note.

• When I first made this recipe, I thought, "Why waste my time thawing frozen peas?" Well, I learned the hard way. If you throw frozen peas into a hot pan, they clump and cook unevenly.

• •

Mushy Minty Peas

Serves 4

First time I saw this on a menu, I was at a pub in London with my friend Julie. I thought, "Yuck. Who would want mushy peas?" I imagined baby food or, worse, hospital food. Being a pea-lover, I ordered it anyway. I'm glad I did because it's been one of my favorite dishes ever since. The peas are mushed, but not actually mushy. I make mine like a coarse puree, and when fresh peas are in season, the texture is even better.

¼ cup heavy cream

Kosher salt

2 cups cooked fresh peas or thawed frozen peas

1 tablespoon finely chopped fresh mint leaves

Freshly ground black pepper

1 Bring the cream and ¼ teaspoon salt to a boil in a large skillet over medium heat. Boil for 2 minutes.

2 Add the peas and mint and stir until heated through. Transfer to a blender or food processor and pulse to puree half of the peas. Season to taste with salt and pepper, and serve immediately.

Serve with simply cooked white fish or roasted meats (pages 142–147).

• •

Carla's Tips

• To chop mint without bruising it, stack the leaves and roll 'em tightly, like a sleeping bag. Slice them very thinly one way with a really sharp knife, then the other way. Don't keep chopping! You gotta get through 'em the first time.

• Mint is a potent herb, but occasionally you get a dud bunch that doesn't taste like much. If that's the case, add more to the dish.

• •

INDIAN

Chile, Pea, and Coconut Chutney

Serves 4

Until I made this dish, I had never had peas so spicy, punchy, and powerful. Imagine a sweet pea puree with hot hits of chile, mellow coconut, and pops of lime. Yeah, it's that awesome. I can't get enough of this easy chutney; I down it by the spoonful!

1½ teaspoons canola oil

½ teaspoon yellow mustard seeds

2 cups cooked fresh peas or thawed frozen peas

2 serrano chiles, stemmed, seeded, and sliced

1 garlic clove, chopped

2 tablespoons shredded unsweetened coconut

2 tablespoons fresh lime juice

½ teaspoon kosher salt

1 Heat the oil in a small skillet over medium heat. Add the mustard seeds and cook, stirring, until golden brown, about 1 minute. Set the skillet aside.

2 In a blender or food processor, pulse the peas, chiles, garlic, coconut, lime juice, and salt until coarsely ground. Add the mustard seeds with the oil, and pulse until mixed in. Serve immediately or refrigerate in an airtight container for up to 1 day.

Serve with grilled shrimp or chicken or with warm naan bread.

• •

Carla's Tips

• You know how mustard's hot? Mustard seeds aren't. Trust me. They have a fantastic mustardy spice and an amazing pop. That little crunch really comes out when they're toasted or fried in oil.

• •

World Peas

I love peas so much, I wanted to explore how they're used all over the globe. When I stumbled across this chutney, I was really intrigued. I never would've thought of these ingredients—chiles, mustard, coconut—for peas and almost didn't expect it to be good. Of course I couldn't resist trying it, especially since it takes only minutes to whip up. When I took a bite, I was hit by what a happy dish this is. The flavors are just so bright and sweet.

To make sure I wasn't the only one who loved this cool combination, I had Genevieve, my writer, and Verlette, my cookie company manager, try it, too. Both of them went crazy for it!

What I really love about this dish is how it sums up what this book is all about: getting a glimpse of how food's prepared elsewhere. This familiar, comforting veggie tastes totally different with Indian flavors. We're on one side of the world, but we can still enjoy a taste of the other side.

Spinach

I love trying leafy greens from other cultures. They vary so widely in their sweet-bitter and tender-crunchy balance, but they all share a fresh green flavor. Spinach is a simple swap here because it's mild, tender, and easy to cook. I've chosen dishes in which the greens are pureed until nearly smooth, so you really taste the global seasonings as much as the greens.

The flavor of fresh bunches from the farmers' market is unbeatable, but I've gotta say, those boxes of triple-washed baby spinach are awesome. The only prep involved is opening the package. And that's important because spinach cooks down like crazy, so you need a lot to feed a few.

If you want to go for good ol' bunches, the best way to wash them is to put them in a salad spinner. Fill the spinner bowl with room-temperature water, swish the greens around, and lift out the colander insert. Rinse out the bowl and repeat at least once. You may have to wash them three or four times before all the grit's gone.

Creamed Spinach

Serves 4

Creamed spinach was kind of a treat when I was growing up. But when I started cooking—and eating—this side dish as an adult, I had trouble finding a version I liked. The cream and greens always felt too separate. I decided to blend the elements to make this beautiful green-on-green dish. It's so quick and easy, I don't have to save it for special occasions.

1 tablespoon unsalted butter

¼ cup finely diced yellow onion

Kosher salt

½ cup heavy cream

1 garlic clove, finely minced

½ teaspoon freshly grated nutmeg

1 pound baby spinach

1 Bring a medium saucepan of water to a boil.

2 In a medium skillet, melt the butter over medium heat. Add the onion and ½ teaspoon salt and cook, stirring occasionally, until the onion is translucent, about 2 minutes. Stir in the cream, bring to a boil, and then stir in the garlic and nutmeg. Reduce the heat and simmer until reduced by a third.

3 Meanwhile, add the spinach to the boiling water and cook, stirring, just until wilted. Drain in a fine-mesh sieve, pressing on the spinach to extract as much liquid as possible.

4 In a blender, combine the cream mixture and ½ cup of the spinach. Puree until smooth. Coarsely chop the remaining spinach, squeezing out more liquid if necessary. Combine the chopped and pureed spinach in the skillet and heat over medium heat until well mixed and hot.

• •

Carla's Tips

• **Squeeze!** Water clings to cooked spinach, so you've got to squeeze it out—hard—before you chop or puree it. (And you've really got to squeeze thawed frozen spinach.) Otherwise, the dish's flavors get watered down.

• •

Palak Paneer: Creamy Spiced Spinach with Fried Cheese

Serves 6

Matthew and I probably order Indian food more than any other cuisine. We each have our favorites, and this is one of mine. One of the coolest things about Indian cooking is the way spices and creaminess mingle. Here, lightly browned cubes of soft, fresh cheese balance the spiced pureed greens perfectly.

Paneer

8 ounces fresh ricotta cheese

Canola oil, as needed

Spinach

3 tablespoons extra virgin olive oil or half oil, half butter

1 medium yellow onion, finely chopped

3 garlic cloves, minced

1/2 teaspoon crushed red chile flakes

1 tablespoon grated peeled fresh ginger

1 teaspoon ground coriander

2 1/2 teaspoons ground cumin

1/2 teaspoon ground turmeric

Kosher salt

1/2 cup sour cream

2 pounds baby spinach

1 large beefsteak tomato, cut into 1-inch wedges

1 tablespoon chopped fresh cilantro leaves

1 To make the paneer: Line a fine-mesh sieve with paper towels and set it over a sturdy bowl. Place the ricotta in the paper towels and press until all the liquid is released and the solids are dry. The ricotta needs to be firm enough to cut. Transfer the pressed cheese to a cutting board and cut it into 1-inch cubes.

2 In a large nonstick skillet, heat 1½ teaspoons canola oil over medium-high heat. Add a single layer of cheese cubes and cook until browned, about 2 minutes per side. Repeat with the remaining cheese cubes, replenishing and reheating the oil between batches; reserve.

3 To make the spinach: Heat the oil over medium heat in a large, deep skillet. Add the onion, garlic, chile flakes, and half of the ginger. Cook, stirring frequently, until the onion is tender, about 5 minutes. Add the coriander, cumin, turmeric, and 1 teaspoon salt. Cook, stirring, for 1 minute.

4 Stir in the sour cream, reduce the heat to low, and simmer for 5 minutes. Add the spinach, a handful at a time, stirring to wilt the leaves before adding the next handful. Transfer the wilted spinach to a blender, along with the tomato, cilantro, and remaining ginger. Puree until finely chopped.

5 Return to the skillet and simmer over medium heat for 10 minutes. Season to taste with salt. Top with the paneer and serve hot.

Serve with Chitrana Peanut-Coconut Rice (page 76) or naan bread.

• •

Carla's Tips

• Paneer is really easy to make, but you may be able to find it in Indian groceries, too. It's fantastic in this dish, but the spinach is still tasty without it.

• **Some Like It Hot:** Add a whole teaspoon of chile flakes.

• •

Calaloo: Crab and Coconut Spinach Stew

Serves 8

My brother-in-law, Gus, is the first person who made this dish for me. And I really, really wanted to like it. He used palm oil and that's definitely an acquired taste, as is the traditional funky dried saltfish he threw in there. This is a dish that hails from my heritage, so I wanted to create my own take on it. I played around with the essential ingredients until I got to this version, which I luuuuuuv. *The savory bacon and crab add a real depth of flavor, and the okra and coconut milk give the stew body. When I took my first bite, I screamed. Literally. It just hit me with its soulfulness and super, super tastiness. I hope you love it as much as I do.*

3 strips bacon

1 large green bell pepper, stemmed, seeded, and cut into ¹/₂-inch dice

1 small yellow onion, finely diced

4 scallions (green onions), trimmed and thinly sliced

4 garlic cloves, minced

Kosher salt

8 okra pods, trimmed and cut into ¹/₂-inch rounds

2 sprigs fresh thyme

1 Scotch bonnet chile, slit open

1 pound king crab legs, cut into individual legs

3 cups Chicken Stock (page 103) or store-bought unsalted chicken broth

1 cup coconut milk

1 pound baby spinach

1 In a large, deep skillet, cook the bacon over medium heat, turning occasionally, until the fat has rendered and the bacon is crisp, about 5 minutes. Drain on paper towels, crumble, and reserve.

2 To the fat in the pan, add the bell pepper, onion, scallions, garlic, and ½ teaspoon salt. Cook, stirring occasionally, until the onion is just translucent, about 2 minutes. Add the okra, thyme, and chile. Cook, stirring occasionally, until the okra is just tender, about 5 minutes.

3 Add the crab legs and cook, stirring, for 2 minutes. Add the chicken stock, coconut milk, and a pinch of salt. Bring to a boil over high heat. Then cover, reduce the heat to a simmer, and cook for 15 minutes.

4 Transfer the crab legs, chile, and thyme sprigs to a dish; discard the chile and thyme.

5 Stir the spinach into the skillet and cook until it wilts, about 1 minute. Transfer to a blender and puree until finely chopped. Season to taste with salt, keeping in mind that both the bacon and the crab are naturally salty. Transfer the pureed spinach to a serving bowl, and top with the bacon and crab legs.

· ·

Carla's Tips

• I like to get my hands dirty when I'm eating. I want the whole crab legs in my spinach so I can pick them up with my fingers and pick and suck the meat and all their savory juices out of the shells. My husband, Matthew? Not so much. I crack the crab for him and pull out all the meat first. That way, he can enjoy the dish with a fork, just the way he likes. You should serve this however you want; it's delicious both ways.

• **Some Like It Hot:** Add another Scotch bonnet chile and smash both into the stew.

· ·

Eggplant

Eggplant flesh is like a sponge that soaks up seasonings.
That's why I chose this versatile veggie to show off cuisines as disparate as Italian and Chinese. Granted, they use different varieties. In Italian-American cooking, globe eggplants, the big guys most readily available in supermarkets, are used. Chinese recipes call for the long, slender varieties with fewer seeds—these hold up well in stir-fries. Nowadays, you can find a wide variety at farmers' markets, from tiny rounds to stripy cylinders. They're worth trying because their tastes and textures do vary a bit.

The one thing I don't like about eggplant is when it gets mushy. To keep the firm texture, I draw the water out of it first. I've given a few different techniques in the recipes that follow. Don't skip this step! It makes a big difference in the cooking.

Spiced Eggplant Stewed with Potatoes and Tomatoes

Serves 4

Everything about this dish goes against the way I usually cook. I like to brown in small batches and preserve the different textures of vegetables. Here, you dump it all in and just let it go. And it's tasty that way! The flavors marry while stewing and are even better the next day. But I do keep a little crunch by using whole cumin seeds, and I toast them, too, to release their natural oils. I love adding that extra layer of flavor to accentuate the ground cumin already in the stew.

3 tablespoons canola oil

1 teaspoon cumin seeds

1 large yellow onion, finely diced

Kosher salt

5 baby eggplants, peeled and cut into
1-inch dice

8 baby Yukon gold potatoes, scrubbed
and cut into 1-inch dice

2 large tomatoes, peeled and cut into
1-inch dice (see Carla's Tips)

1½ teaspoons ground coriander

¼ teaspoon ground turmeric

½ teaspoon cayenne pepper

1½ teaspoons ground cumin

1 Heat the oil in a large Dutch oven or flameproof casserole over medium-high heat. Add the cumin seeds and let them sizzle until fragrant and golden brown, about 1 minute. Add the onion and 1 teaspoon salt and cook, stirring occasionally, until the onion is almost translucent, about 3 minutes.

2 Add the eggplant, potatoes, and 1 teaspoon salt. Cook, stirring, until the vegetables are starting to color, about 5 minutes. Stir in the tomatoes, coriander, turmeric, cayenne, and ground cumin.

3 Bring to a boil, then cover and reduce the heat to a simmer. Cook until the potatoes are tender, about 25 minutes.

Serve with Chitrana Peanut-Coconut Rice (page 76) or warm naan bread.

• •

Carla's Tips

• To peel the tomatoes: Fill a bowl with ice and water. Bring a small saucepan of water to a boil. Use a sharp knife to cut an "x" at the bottom of each tomato. Carefully lower them into the boiling water, and as soon as the skin gapes at the "x," transfer them to the ice water with a slotted spoon. Peel and discard the skins. You can also peel the tomatoes with a sharp serrated peeler.

• **Some Like It Hot:** Double the cayenne.

• •

Caponata: Eggplant, Tomato, and Raisin Relish

Serves 4

I had no idea what caponata was until I went to culinary school, and then I was seeing it everywhere! It's like buying a car that you never even knew existed and then spying one at every corner. Caponata is basically an eggplant dish where the sweetness of tomatoes and raisins is balanced by the saltiness of capers and olives. It all comes together with a tart dose of vinegar. There are countless variations, but I make mine with texture, keeping the celery crisp, the raisins chewy, and the nuts crunchy. I once had an absolutely delicious mushy version, but it wasn't good enough to make me want to change mine.

1 large globe eggplant, peeled and cut into ½-inch chunks

Kosher salt

3 tablespoons plus 1 teaspoon extra virgin olive oil

1 medium yellow onion, diced

2 garlic cloves, minced

4 plum tomatoes, diced

1 sprig fresh oregano

3 large celery ribs, diced

2 tablespoons pine nuts, toasted

2 tablespoons golden raisins

2 tablespoons capers, rinsed and drained

5 green olives, pitted and cut into thin slivers

¼ cup red wine vinegar

2 teaspoons sugar

2 tablespoons chopped fresh parsley leaves

1 Toss the eggplant with 1 teaspoon salt and let it sit in a colander to drain while the other vegetables cook, about 20 minutes.

2 Meanwhile, heat 2 tablespoons of the oil in a large skillet over medium-high heat. Add the onion and ½ teaspoon salt and cook, stirring, until the onion is a little tender and lightly browned, about 3 minutes. Add the garlic and cook, stirring, for 2 minutes. Add the tomatoes and oregano and stir well. Bring to a boil, then reduce the heat to a simmer and cook until thick and pasty, about 30 minutes.

3 While the tomatoes simmer, toss the celery with the 1 teaspoon oil. Heat another skillet over high heat. Add the celery and ¼ teaspoon salt, and spread out in a single layer. Cook, tossing, until translucent, about 4 minutes. Transfer to a plate and spread out to stop the cooking.

4 Squeeze the eggplant dry between paper towels, and then toss it with the remaining 1 tablespoon oil. Add some of the eggplant to the same hot skillet in a single layer. Cook, tossing occasionally, until browned, about 2 minutes. Transfer it to a plate and repeat with the remaining eggplant, working in batches.

5 Stir the celery, eggplant, pine nuts, raisins, capers, olives, vinegar, sugar, and parsley into the tomatoes. Discard the oregano sprig. Serve immediately or refrigerate in an airtight container for up to 1 week.

Serve cold or warm, with fish or crusty Italian bread.

Carla's Tips

• Salting the eggplant first draws out its moisture, which helps it brown in the skillet. It also removes any bitterness.

• Is it worth getting an extra skillet dirty just to sauté the celery and eggplant? Absolutely. A quick sauté takes off the raw edge of the celery, but keeps it crisp in the relish; the hot skillet also browns the eggplant, preventing it from turning to mush in the tomatoes.

CHINESE

Hot and Sour Eggplant Stir-fry

Serves 4

One summer, I catered alongside my friend Anna Saint John at the Washington Ballet School summer camp. She made this spicy eggplant basil dip that combined the heat of chiles with the sweetness of the vegetables. Inspired by that puree, I re-created the original Chinese version since I love its variety of textures. Here, the eggplant's skin blisters while the flesh gets tender. Stir-fries are all ticky-boo (my term for dishes in which the cooking goes super fast and has to be done at the last minute, right before serving), so be sure to have all your ingredients ready before you start cooking.

5 small, stripy eggplants or Chinese or Japanese eggplants, trimmed, cut in eighths lengthwise, then cut in halves crosswise

Kosher salt

3 quarts warm water

2 serrano chiles, stemmed and minced, with seeds

1 tablespoon sugar

1½ tablespoons soy sauce

1 tablespoon red wine vinegar

1 teaspoon cornstarch

2 tablespoons canola oil

2 scallions (green onions), trimmed and cut into 1-inch pieces

2 tablespoons sliced fresh basil leaves

1 Sprinkle the eggplant pieces with 1 tablespoon salt, then immerse in the warm water in a large bowl. Let stand while you prepare the other ingredients.

2 In a small bowl, stir the chiles, sugar, soy sauce, vinegar, and cornstarch until the sugar dissolves.

3 Drain the eggplant very well and press dry between paper towels. Heat a wok or large skillet over high heat until very hot. Add 1 tablespoon of the oil, then add half of the eggplant. Cook, tossing and stirring, until browned and just tender, about 5 minutes. Transfer to a plate. Repeat with the remaining oil and eggplant, and then return the first batch of eggplant to the wok.

4 Add the scallions and the chile mixture. Cook, tossing and stirring, for 2 minutes. Toss in the basil and serve immediately.

Serve with Perfect Baked Rice (page 71).

. . . .

Carla's Tips

• Soaking the eggplant in warm water, then squeezing it dry before cooking, helps the flesh stay intact during high-heat stir-frying.

• If you don't have a huge wok and a crazy-hot flame, cook the eggplant in batches to make sure it browns properly. I timed it and found that you don't save any time not cooking in batches because it takes longer for a big batch to cook through.

. . . .

Corn

I've gone all New World flavors here, to celebrate corn's native home.
I grew up on Southern preparations that either kept the corn kernels crunchy and fresh
or cooked 'em to creamy comfort. I love those mellow treatments as much as I do the
spicy ones south of the border. The key to both is getting great corn. Heirloom varieties
straight from the farm have amazing, complex flavors, but even supermarket ears can be
nice. Any time of year other than summer, know that the corn will be more starchy and
less sweet. Look for ears with plump kernels that are tightly packed in rows, whether
they're yellow, white, some shade in between, or a combination.

Butter Up! Tangy Spicy Butter

The only thing fresh summer corn needs is a nice slather of butter. But I like to take it one step further by seasoning the butter. Herb blends are great, but this is my new favorite. Bright lime brings out the fruitiness of habanero chiles and cuts through the milky richness of butter. You can use this tangy-spicy butter on just about anything. Grilled sweet potatoes, chicken, steak, and meaty fish like tuna are favorites, and it's awesome melted into boiled white potatoes, but I like it best with grilled corn. This makes enough butter for 16 ears of corn, but you can cut off a chunk and use a little at a time. If you want to make less, scale it down proportionally. The smallest batch you could do is ¼ cup butter, ¼ chile, ¼ teaspoon lime zest, ¾ teaspoon lime juice, and a small pinch of salt. And if you want it even hotter, simply keep the seeds in the chile.

- ½ pound (2 sticks) unsalted butter, at room temperature

- 1 habanero chile, stemmed, seeded, and minced

- 1 teaspoon freshly grated lime zest

- 1 tablespoon fresh lime juice

- ¾ teaspoon kosher salt

In a large bowl, stir and mash all the ingredients until very well mixed. Spoon the seasoned butter in a line on a sheet of parchment or wax paper, and then use the paper to roll the butter into a log. Refrigerate until firm or up to 1 week. You can also freeze it for up to 1 month.

 SOUTHERN

Baked Corn Pudding

Serves 12

This is the ultimate entertaining dish. I used it for catering all the time because it's a big casserole of yummy comfort that everyone loves, and it tastes great even when made ahead. One of my former catering cooks, Chin, always nailed this recipe. She was known as the catering goddess in the D.C. area because she could pull off feats like bangin' out trays and trays of this dish while carefully stirring each one to get the corn suspended evenly throughout each pudding. It's that one detail that really makes this dish.

3 tablespoons unsalted butter, melted, plus more for the dish

4 large eggs

4 teaspoons sugar

1 teaspoon kosher salt

¼ cup all-purpose flour

¼ cup fine stone-ground cornmeal

3 cups whole milk

1 cup heavy cream

4 cups fresh corn kernels

1 Preheat the oven to 450°F. Butter a shallow 3-quart baking dish.

2 In a large bowl, vigorously whisk the eggs until fluffy. Whisk in the sugar and salt until dissolved, then whisk in the flour and cornmeal until blended. Whisk in the milk, cream, and melted butter. Pour into the baking dish and scatter the corn kernels evenly over the top. (They'll sink.)

3 Bake for 20 minutes. Drag (do not stir) a fork through the pudding from end to end to make sure all the corn kernels don't settle at the bottom. Reduce the oven temperature to 350°F and bake until just set, about 20 minutes. Serve hot, warm, or at room temperature.

. . . .

Carla's Tips

• Stone-ground corn sounds all rustic—and I guess it is—but it's actually ground finer than regular cornmeal. Be sure to buy it to keep this pudding's texture light and fluffy.

. . . .

Esquites: Quick Sautéed Corn with Jalapeño

Serves 4

When I first had Mexican-style street corn—charred corn on the cob slathered with mayo, cheese, spices, herbs, and lime juice—at a taqueria in California, all I could say was "Oh. My. God. Shut the front door. This is so good!" It became one of my favorite super tasty and super messy street foods. When I want those flavors in a sit-down meal, I do these esquites instead. Same creamy and bright flavors, but in a quick skillet dish that's pretty enough for company.

1 tablespoon unsalted butter

1 jalapeño chile, stemmed and minced,
   with seeds

Kosher salt

1/2 teaspoon dried oregano

3 cups fresh corn kernels

1/2 cup Chicken Stock (page 103) or
   store-bought unsalted chicken broth

Crema or sour cream, for serving

Crumbled cotija or feta cheese, for serving

Lime wedges, for serving

Ground Mexican chile, such as ancho,
   for serving

1 In a large skillet, melt the butter over medium-high heat. Add the jalapeño and a pinch of salt. Cook, stirring, for 1 minute. Add the oregano and cook, stirring, for 30 seconds. Add the corn and cook, stirring, for 1 minute.

2 Stir in the stock and 1/2 teaspoon salt and bring to a boil. Reduce the heat to a simmer and cook until the corn is crisp-tender, about 5 minutes.

3 Top with crema, cotija, a squirt of lime juice, and a sprinkling of ground chile. Serve hot.

• •

Carla's Tips

• The very best way to make this dish is to simmer the chicken stock with the corn cobs from which you cut the kernels for 30 minutes before adding it to the sauté.

• If you want to re-create the smokiness of grilled corn, sprinkle it with some smoked paprika in addition to the chile.

• •

 ALL-AMERICAN

Sweet Corn and Tomato Relish

Serves 4

This is one of those salads that's only as good as its ingredients. So, summer's the season for this easy toss. Ideally, you'd pluck your tomatoes warm from the garden the way my Granny used to, but if you can't do that, look for juicy ripe ones at farmers' markets. And pick up some pretty ears of corn while you're there. I promise to tell you when you can substitute canned or frozen vegetables for fresh ones. This isn't one of those places.

4 ears corn, husks and silks removed

2 tablespoons extra virgin olive oil, plus more for grilling the corn

1 large tomato, peeled, cored, seeded, and finely diced (see Carla's Tips)

1/2 small red onion, very finely diced

1 jalapeño chile, stemmed, seeded, and finely chopped

2 small garlic cloves, finely minced

Grated zest and juice of 1 lime

1 teaspoon ground cumin

1/2 teaspoon kosher salt

1 tablespoon fresh cilantro leaves, coarsely chopped

1 Heat a grill on high heat until very hot. Rub the corn with enough oil to lightly coat. Grill, turning occasionally, until blackened in spots and starting to pop, about 5 minutes. Don't overcook! The corn should still be yellow and have a bite. Transfer to a plate and let cool.

2 When they are cool enough to handle, lay each ear of corn on its side and cut off one side of kernels. Rotate the cob and cut off another side of kernels. Keep rotating and cutting until all the kernels are off.

3 Transfer the kernels to a large bowl, and add the tomato, onion, jalapeño, garlic, lime zest and juice, cumin, salt, and 2 tablespoons oil. Toss until well mixed. Garnish with the cilantro.

Serve with Burgers 101 (page 126) or grilled fish or chicken.

• •

Carla's Tips

• When I was developing recipes for this book, I was shocked to see my co-author, Genevieve, turn an ear of corn on its side to cut off the kernels. I was like, "What?!" Then I tried it . . . and I've been doing it that way since. No more trying to slice wobbly upright ears of corn.

• To peel the tomato: Fill a bowl with ice and water. Bring a small saucepan of water to a boil. Use a sharp knife to cut an "x" in the bottom of the tomato. Carefully lower it into the boiling water, and as soon as the skin gapes at the "x," transfer it to the ice water with a slotted spoon. Peel and discard the skin. You can also peel the tomato with a sharp serrated peeler.

• •

Green Beans

Yes, green beans can be great raw . . . and even what some might call overcooked. I never say never when trying dishes and have figured out a way to make classic super-soft American green beans great. On the other end of the spectrum, I've kept them crunchy as pickles. And right in the middle, I've blazed them in a hot oven.

For all of my rustic treatments, be sure to start with good ol' American beans and not the slender, forest-green French haricots verts. I wash my beans well first, in case there's any grit, then I tip and tail them. While I find it therapeutic to snap both ends one by one, ideally on a sunny porch, I often don't have time for that. The fastest way to trim green beans is to bunch up a handful and line up their stem ends, then slice straight across. I like to do the tails too: line up the other ends and cut off those little suckers.

 ITALIAN

Roasted Green Beans with Basil

Serves 4

My motto for roasting green beans: the hotter, the quicker, the better. They get nice and charred and there's great flavor in that brown. If there's anything I've learned about Italian food from my Chew *co-host Mario Batali, it's that vegetables should be treated simply to let their natural sweetness shine. This recipe does just that.*

1 pound green beans, trimmed

8 garlic cloves, unpeeled, ends trimmed

3 tablespoons extra virgin olive oil

1 small yellow onion, cut in half and then into ¼-inch-thick half-moons

Kosher salt

¼ cup sliced fresh basil leaves

1 teaspoon fresh lemon juice

1 Preheat the oven to 450°F. Toss the green beans and garlic cloves with 2 tablespoons of the oil on a rimmed baking sheet. Arrange them in a single layer on one side of the pan. Arrange the onion slices in a single layer on the other side of the pan and rub with the remaining 1 tablespoon oil. Sprinkle ½ teaspoon salt over everything. Roast until the green beans are browned and tender, about 25 minutes.

2 Squeeze the garlic cloves out of their skins into a large bowl, and mash them. Then add the green beans, onions, basil, and ¼ teaspoon salt. Toss well, then toss in the lemon juice and serve.

 ALL-AMERICAN

Cooked-to-Death-Delicious Green Beans with Potatoes

Serves 4

As a chef, I learned to never overcook green beans. I carefully watched pots so that the beans wouldn't go from perfectly crisp-tender to squeaky soft. But I've reclaimed my Granny's cooked-to-death green beans. The key is to get past that stage where the green beans are overcooked and still have a little bite to the point where they're so overcooked, they're totally tender.

2 teaspoons rendered bacon fat

1 large yellow onion, cut in half and very thinly sliced

Kosher salt

2 garlic cloves, sliced

¼ teaspoon crushed red chile flakes

3 cups Chicken Stock (page 103) or store-bought unsalted chicken broth

1½ pounds small Yukon gold potatoes (about 18), scrubbed, a strip peeled from each

1 pound green beans, trimmed

1 Heat the bacon fat in a 5-quart saucepan over medium-high heat. Add the onion and ½ teaspoon salt. Cook, stirring occasionally, until just tender, about 2 minutes. Add the garlic and chile flakes and cook, stirring frequently, until the onion is tender, about 3 minutes.

2 Add the stock, potatoes, and ½ teaspoon salt. Bring to a boil, then reduce the heat to maintain a steady simmer. Simmer until the potatoes are just tender enough to be pierced with a fork but are still firm, about 20 minutes.

3 Add the green beans, cover, and simmer until they are very tender, about 10 minutes. Use a slotted spoon to transfer the potatoes and green beans to a serving dish. Bring the liquid to a boil and boil until reduced to 1 cup, about 6 minutes. Spoon over the vegetables and gently fold to mix. Serve hot.

• •

Carla's Tips

• Here's how Granny always peeled her spuds for this dish: She removed just one strip of peel, the width of the peeler, around the center of each potato. So the rounds are naked in the middle but have caps of peel on two ends.

• If you don't have rendered bacon fat on hand, cook 4 strips to get the fat needed in this recipe. You can then crumble the cooked bacon on top at the end.

• •

Pickled Green Beans

Makes 2 quarts

One summer, I got into a pickling frenzy. It started with Tangy Chow Chow Pickles (page 56) and quickly moved on to this Southern staple. Although some recipes call for cooking the green beans first, I prefer to use them raw so that they become snappy pickles.

2 pounds green beans, trimmed

4 garlic cloves, peeled

1½ cups white vinegar

3 cups water

¼ cup kosher salt

¼ cup sugar

1 tablespoon celery seeds or dill seeds

½ teaspoon crushed red chile flakes

1 Divide the green beans and garlic between two sterilized 1-quart canning jars.

2 Combine the vinegar, water, salt, and sugar in a medium saucepan. Bring to a boil, stirring to dissolve the salt and sugar. Boil for 1 minute, then remove from the heat and stir in the celery seeds and chile flakes. Ladle the mixture over the green beans, and jar properly or refrigerate for up to 3 months. You can serve this within 2 weeks.

Serve with Hot Fried Chicken (page 112) or other rich dishes.

Carla's Tips

• If you're using four 1-pint jars, trim the green beans so that they'll be ¼ inch below the rim.

• I love my pickles pucker-my-lips tangy, but if you prefer 'em sweeter, increase the sugar.

Cauliflower

Its mildness is what makes cauliflower great for my style of cooking with big, deep flavors. This pale cruciferous vegetable takes to just about any seasoning, so I load it up with my favorite combos. Look for heads that are unblemished, with leaves tightly tucked under the compact florets. Snap off the leaves, then trim the thick bottom stem before prepping. The real key to good cauliflower is to start by cooking it properly. Undercooked and it'll be hard; overcooked and it gets that smelly funk. A cake tester or a sharp, thin knife works best for checking doneness. It should slide through the stem with just a hint of resistance.

 INDIAN

Spiced Roasted Cauliflower

Serves 4

When I think Indian food, I think spice. So the first time I did this dish, I went a little overboard and I learned that Indian food is about spice, but not about hitting you over the head with it. Now I've got the balance just right for cauliflower that's been thrown into a super-hot oven where its natural sweetness intensifies as the florets caramelize. After my initial misfire on this dish, I also found that a combo of butter and oil works best: The butter adds richness and the oil helps the browning. This blend delivers the fragrant flavors of the spices, making it ideal for any roasted vegetables.

1 teaspoon garam masala

1/2 teaspoon cumin seeds

1/4 teaspoon ground coriander

1/4 teaspoon cayenne pepper

2 tablespoons unsalted butter

2 tablespoons canola oil

Kosher salt

1 large (2 1/2-pound) cauliflower, cored and cut into small florets

Lime wedges

1 Preheat the oven to 425°F. Combine the garam masala, cumin, coriander, and cayenne in a small skillet. Toast over medium-high heat, shaking the skillet occasionally, until fragrant, 1 to 2 minutes. Remove from the heat and add the butter, oil, and 1 teaspoon salt. Stir until the butter melts.

2 Toss the cauliflower with the spiced butter on a rimmed baking sheet until well coated. Spread the cauliflower out in a single layer and roast until tender and browned, about 15 minutes. Season to taste with salt and lime juice.

Broiled Cauliflower Steaks with Olive Relish

Serves 6

Doing cauliflower as steaks has become a pretty trendy thing. I've made them for years, but the most memorable version was one my Chew *co-host Mario Batali did at a fundraiser. Mario knew Bill Clinton would be there, so he created a main course to suit the ex-president's vegan diet. Mario's mushroom garnish over crisp brown cauliflower was so delicious and satisfying! But what I loved most about that dish was how it highlighted Mario's thoughtfulness as a chef. As a caterer and hostess, I always wanted to make vegan options to show vegetarians and vegans that I care. This savory dish is pretty and tasty enough to do just that.*

2 medium (2-pound) cauliflowers

6 tablespoons extra virgin olive oil

Kosher salt

3 garlic cloves, finely chopped

¼ teaspoon crushed red chile flakes

3 tablespoons chopped fresh oregano leaves

2 tablespoons capers, rinsed, drained, and chopped

2 tablespoons pitted Kalamata olives, chopped

1 lemon

1 Arrange the broiler rack 6 inches from the heat source. Preheat the broiler.

2 Remove the leaves from the cauliflowers, then cut each one into ½-inch-thick slices from top to bottom, keeping the core intact. You should get 3 "steaks" from each cauliflower and florets from the ends.

3 Coat a rimmed baking sheet with 1 tablespoon of the oil and arrange the cauliflower steaks and florets in a single layer in the pan. Drizzle with 2 tablespoons of the oil and sprinkle with ½ teaspoon salt. Broil until the tops have browned, about 8 minutes. Then carefully flip the pieces and broil until the other side is browned and the cauliflower is tender, about 5 minutes.

4 Meanwhile, heat the remaining 3 tablespoons oil in a small skillet over low heat. Add the garlic and cook for 30 seconds, shaking the pan. Then add the chile flakes and cook for 15 seconds, shaking the pan. Add the oregano and remove from the heat. Stir in the capers and olives. Just before serving, zest the lemon directly over the mixture and stir well. Spoon over the broiled cauliflower and serve immediately.

• •

Carla's Tips

• Use a big, wide spatula to flip the cauliflower steaks. It helps keep the branches from falling apart.

• •

Real Recipe Research

When I started cooking, the internet wasn't what it is now. I couldn't find millions of recipes to try out in a keystroke. (Believe it, kids.) I relied on expertly written cookbooks and I consulted chefs. Sometimes I didn't have those resources on hand, either. Like the time I had to do a last-minute St. Patrick's Day dinner at the Henley Park Hotel.

I was new there and faced with creating a holiday meal for a culture I didn't really know. But I did know an Irishman named Tony. He was the smoked salmon salesman for the restaurant and was always very friendly to me. I asked, "Tony! What should I make for the St. Paddy's Day dinner?" He replied in his thick Irish brogue, "Soda bread, of course, and corned beef and colcannon." That was my research. I scoured my cookbooks for those dishes and made them that night. Everything came out well, but the colcannon was my personal favorite. I'm a sucker for mashed potatoes and I loved the addition of scallions. I swapped the traditional cabbage for cauliflower to lighten the texture and have stuck with my version ever since.

At that point in my career, I wasn't afraid to try new things and serve them. (And there were some real failures.) It didn't even cross my mind to test recipes over and over again. It didn't take long for me to see the value in perfecting recipes for paying customers, but I keep that spirit of adventure in the kitchen. If you hear of a dish you've never tasted, through the internet or through good old-fashioned conversations, you should go ahead and try it. You never know—you may just find a new favorite.

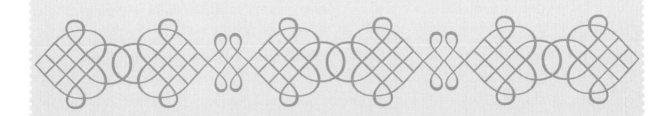

IRISH

Colcannon: Cauliflower, Potato, and Scallion Mash

Serves 8

Cauliflower gets super creamy when mashed into floury potatoes and, well, cream. As much as I love plain ol' mashed potatoes, I also love the earthy sweetness of this mix and the way the cauliflower lightens the texture of starchy potatoes. I know colcannon is traditionally made with cabbage, but I've never done it that way. I prefer to season it with the mellow punch of garlic and scallions . . . and a side of corned beef.

2½ pounds russet potatoes, peeled and cut into quarters

Kosher salt

1 large (2½-pound) cauliflower, cored and cut into 1-inch florets

1 cup heavy cream

1 cup milk

2 garlic cloves, peeled and smashed

2 bunches scallions (green onions), trimmed and finely chopped

3 tablespoons unsalted butter, at room temperature

Freshly ground black pepper

1 Place the potatoes in a large pot and add enough cold water to cover by 2 inches. Generously salt the water and bring to a boil over high heat. Cover, reduce the heat to a simmer, and cook until the potatoes are just tender enough to pierce with a fork, about 12 minutes.

2 Add the cauliflower and cook, uncovered, until both the potatoes and cauliflower are very tender, about 10 minutes.

3 Meanwhile, in a small saucepan, heat the cream, milk, garlic, and ½ teaspoon salt until warmed, about 5 minutes. Mash the garlic into the hot cream.

4 Drain the potatoes and cauliflower and return to the pot. Let stand until dry, about 5 minutes, then mash in the scallions, hot cream mixture, and butter. Season to taste with salt and pepper.

Serve with any meaty roast or stew.

• •

Carla's Tips

• You can use 2 cups half-and-half here instead of the milk-cream combo.

• You gotta let the cooked veggies dry out a bit before mashing in the liquids. Otherwise, you'll dilute their flavors.

• •

Butternut Squash

Winter squash feels so American to me, but I've found a wide variety from all over the world that ranges from deep red to pale orange, from dense and meaty to watery and stringy. Butternut's a solid, middle-of-the-road squash that's easily found in markets. I've found that its combo of sweet and starch makes it ideal in other cuisines, too. It gets so naturally sugary when cooked, it tastes like a universal treat. Choose ones with smooth skin that feel heavy for their size. I always look for long ones without too much of a bulbous bottom because they're much easier to peel and cut. Sometimes, I feel a little lazy in the kitchen, too!

 ITALIAN

Roasted Garlic and Chile Butternut Squash
Serves 8

When I first developed this dish, I was worried I wasn't adding enough seasonings. I was trying to stay true to the Italian spirit of keeping vegetables simple to let them shine. Then I nibbled a half-moon of squash. Boom! It was so, so good. That hint of garlic-chile heat brought out all the natural sweetness of the squash.

1 large butternut squash, trimmed, peeled, cut in half lengthwise, seeds and strings discarded

2 tablespoons extra virgin olive oil

1 teaspoon kosher salt

5 garlic cloves, peeled and smashed

¼ teaspoon crushed red chile flakes

1 Preheat the oven to 350°F. Cut the squash crosswise into ½-inch-thick half-moons. Transfer to a rimmed baking sheet and toss with the oil, salt, garlic, and chile flakes. Spread out in a single layer.

2 Roast the squash until tender and browned, about 30 minutes.

Carla's Tips

• A strong vegetable peeler's good for removing the thick skin of butternut squash.

• **Some Like It Hot:** Add more crushed red chile flakes or even a pinch of cayenne.

THAI

Butternut Squash with Coconut Sauce

Serves 8

Two cultures connect in this dish. When I tasted the Italian-inspired Roasted Garlic and Chile Butternut Squash (page 50), I realized that those basic flavors could work in many different cultures. I decided to go Thai because I love the flavors of that cuisine. The coconut sauce here is simply spooned over the squash and would taste awesome on other vegetables, such as green beans and sweet potatoes.

1 (13.5-ounce) can coconut milk

1 lemongrass stalk (white and pale yellow parts only), smashed and chopped

One 1-inch piece fresh ginger, peeled and chopped

1 garlic clove, chopped

2 fresh Thai chiles

2 strips lime zest, removed with a vegetable peeler

1 teaspoon coriander seeds

¼ teaspoon kosher salt

Roasted Garlic and Chile Butternut Squash (page 50)

1 lime, cut into wedges

Sliced fresh cilantro leaves, for serving

Sliced scallions (green onions), for serving

Carla's Tips

• Spoon this aromatic coconut sauce over other vegetables, chicken, shrimp, or fish, too!

• Use the blunt edge of a chef's knife to smash the tough lemongrass stalk. It helps soften it for chopping and releases its grassy citrus fragrance.

1 In a medium saucepan, combine the coconut milk, lemongrass, ginger, garlic, chiles, lime zest, coriander seeds, and salt. Bring to a boil, then reduce the heat to maintain a simmer and cook until reduced by half. Strain through a fine-mesh sieve, and discard the solids.

2 Arrange the squash on a serving dish, overlapping the pieces slightly. Squirt lime juice all over the squash, then spoon the sauce on top. Garnish with the cilantro and scallions.

Mix and Match

After college, I took a graduation trip to Asia that included a stop in Bangkok. I wasn't really into food then, so I couldn't appreciate the amazing dishes I tasted there. I do remember mistaking a hot Thai green chile for a green bean and chewing right into it. It burned my mouth out! I took a huge swig of icy beer from my friend's bottle to try to tame the heat. I had never had a sip of alcohol in my life (and I still don't drink), but I was willing to do anything to cool down my mouth.

It's funny looking back on that because I can handle—and love—really spicy foods now and because I know in retrospect that I should've reached for a spoonful of rice or something with dairy in it to tame the heat. Over the years, I've also learned to prepare Thai dishes with the seasonings that define them and I've cooked with those flavors enough to create my own dishes, as with the Butternut Squash with Coconut Sauce (opposite). The sauce is decidedly Thai, but it works really well on Italian Roasted Garlic and Chile Butternut Squash (page 50). I hope this book will help you do the same: create sauces and seasonings from one cuisine and put them with something else. You may just stumble upon something really tasty.

Pickles & Preserves

Canning has been all the rage in the food world in recent years, and I love that we've come full circle with pickles and preserves. The technique's nothing new, of course. In fact, it's really old. My ancestors practiced it for generations because it was the best (and cheapest!) way to save summer produce. Granny always turned her garden abundance into pickles and jams. During harvest season, she would swap veggies and fruits with neighbors and they would all make jars and jars of their favorite preserves. I'm passing along a few of those family treasures and introducing a few new ones I've developed with inspiration from other parts of the world.

To safely and properly pickle, be sure to check out the USDA guidelines and follow them carefully.

Pickles

I'm all about tart, and homemade pickles are an awesome way to get my hit of sour crunch. You can pickle just about anything. I love my veggie blends here, but you can mix it up with your favorite seasonal produce too. As a bonus, the acid helps preserve the vegetables, though you should still follow safe canning guidelines when jarring these.

Tangy Chow Chow Pickles

Makes about 3 quarts

My Aunt Bessie, my daddy's sister, used to make this every fall in Nashville. It was her tradition to take everything from her garden and turn it into this mix. I love the different colors here and hope you can find a range of beauties in your garden or local farmers' markets for this goes-with-everything pickle relish. Me? I eat it by the spoonful and I love it on hot dogs!

4 cups finely chopped cabbage

3 cups diced green tomatoes

2½ cups diced bell peppers, preferably a mix of colors

2½ cups diced white onions

½ cup minced jalapeño chiles

⅓ cup kosher salt

2 cups cider vinegar

1 cup water

½ cup sugar

2 tablespoons yellow mustard seeds

1 teaspoon celery seeds

1½ teaspoons ground turmeric

1 In a large bowl, toss the cabbage, tomatoes, peppers, onions, chiles, and salt well with your hands. Cover and refrigerate for at least 4 hours and up to overnight.

2 Meanwhile, in a medium saucepan off the heat, stir together the vinegar, water, sugar, mustard seeds, celery seeds, and turmeric until the sugar dissolves. You can let the mixture sit as long as the vegetables do.

3 Drain the vegetable mixture in a colander, then rinse and drain again.

4 Bring the vinegar mixture to a boil in a large saucepan. Add the vegetables, return to a boil, then reduce the heat and simmer for 5 minutes (you want to keep the crunch). Ladle the mixture into sterilized canning jars and jar properly or refrigerate for up to 3 months. You can serve the chow chow after a day or two.

Serve with everything! I love it with anything Southern.

GERMAN

Quick Fresh Sauerkraut

Makes about 2 quarts

When I first arrived at college, I was fascinated by the little hot dog cart parked across the street from my dorm. I had never seen one in Nashville. I decided to try a dog and got the works: brown mustard, saucy red onions, and sauerkraut. It was so good! I don't think I had even tasted sauerkraut before that. From that day on, I'd go back and get the dog with just the sauerkraut. I knew I had to do a version of that for this book. Real German sauerkraut requires salting fresh cabbage until it wilts and ferments. To get something close to that in a fraction of the time, I cook the cabbage before jarring it. Classic sauerkraut is nothing more than cabbage and salt, but I added caraway seeds here because that little spice has so much character. Of course, this gets even tastier over time.

This quick 'kraut is great with hot dogs. I would know: After creating the recipe, I kept buying hot dogs and buns in order to finish up the jar!

2 tablespoons canola oil

1 medium yellow onion, very thinly sliced

Kosher salt

3 quarts very thinly sliced cabbage

1 tablespoon caraway seeds, toasted

1 1/2 cups water

1 1/4 cups cider vinegar

1 Heat the oil in a large, deep skillet over medium heat. Add the onion and 1 teaspoon salt and cook, stirring occasionally, until the onion starts to soften, about 3 minutes. Stir in the cabbage, caraway seeds, water, vinegar, and 4 teaspoons salt.

2 Bring to a boil while mixing well. Then reduce the heat, cover, and simmer until the cabbage has wilted but is still crisp, about 8 minutes.

3 Ladle the mixture into sterilized canning jars and jar properly or refrigerate for up to 3 months. You can serve it within a day or two.

Serve with hot dogs, sausages, or anything porky or smoky or meaty.

Sweet & Savory Preserves

Jelly's nice and all, but I want preserves with texture. In all of my mixes, I either keep the fruit in chunks or only lightly mash them. If you like smoother jams, mash 'em more. Be sure to start with tasty fruit here. Your jam's only gonna be as good as the ingredients you start with.

 ITALIAN

Roasted Plum Tomato Jam

Makes about 2 cups

Even though I'm using Italian flavors here, I first made this jam in Texas. My friend Tiffany Derry, whom I got to know as a fellow contestant on Top Chef *and* Top Chef: All Stars, *invited me to cook at her Dallas restaurant. Tiffany is all about seasonal cooking, so I decided to do a kind of throwback combo of grilled cheese with tomato soup. This yummy jam went into the sandwiches and really made the meal. It's also tasty on other sandwiches, with any good bread, or slathered on a juicy hunk of grilled meat or fish. It's got the perfect balance of tangy and sweet.*

2 pounds ripe plum tomatoes, cut in half lengthwise

3 garlic cloves, sliced

2 tablespoons extra virgin olive oil

2 teaspoons sugar

2 teaspoons balsamic vinegar

1 sprig fresh thyme, coarsely chopped

1 sprig fresh rosemary, coarsely chopped

Kosher salt and freshly ground black pepper

1 Preheat the oven to 300°F. On a rimmed baking sheet, toss the tomatoes with the garlic, oil, sugar, vinegar, thyme, rosemary, and a generous pinch each of salt and pepper. Spread the tomatoes out in a single layer, cut sides up. Bake until they are shriveled and lightly browned, about 2 hours.

2 When the tomatoes are cool enough to handle, slip off and discard the skins. Discard the thyme and rosemary.

3 Transfer the tomatoes and all the pan juices to a large saucepan. Cook over low heat, mashing occasionally, until the mixture is thick and jammy, about 30 minutes. Ladle it into sterilized jars, and jar properly or refrigerate for up to 3 months.

• •

Carla's Tips

• For a lighter-colored jam, use white balsamic vinegar instead of the usual dark.

• •

 ALL-AMERICAN

Spiced Plum Jam

Makes about 6 cups

Jam is quintessentially American to me, even when I add Asian spices. The lime and anise here work really well with tart red plums. And I feel pretty strongly about the plums: Damson or dark purple plums are too sweet for this mix. Well, I guess you could use purple plums if you want, but don't invite me over to that party!

9 cups large-diced pitted ripe red plums from 12 large (3 1/3 pounds) (do not peel)

2 cups sugar

6 strips lime zest, removed with a vegetable peeler

1/4 cup fresh lime juice

2 whole star anise pods

1 teaspoon kosher salt

1 In a large saucepan, bring the plums, sugar, lime zest and juice, star anise, and salt to a boil, stirring to dissolve the sugar. Adjust the heat to a simmer and cook for 30 minutes.

2 Use a potato masher to lightly mash the fruit. Discard the star anise. Ladle the mixture into sterilized canning jars and jar properly or refrigerate for up to 3 months.

• •

Carla's Tips

• If you can't find the star anise in the cooked jam, leave it in. It'll turn up eventually . . . just don't eat it!

• •

The Best PB&J

When I worked as a caterer, I was like the shoemaker's kid who didn't have any shoes. I'd prepare all this fancy food, but I wouldn't eat any of it. Honestly, I didn't even *feel* like eating it. Instead, I'd buy the fixins for PB&J after a long day of cooking. That was the comfort I craved.

Safeway had this one brand of plum jam that I loved. It was as tart as sour cherry jam, but with this distinct plummy-ness that made it feel like the end of summer any time of the year.

I haven't been able to find it on the shelves for years, so I've created my own version. I think I've managed to capture the tastes of late summer. Best of all, I now have the makings for my ideal PB&J.

INDIAN

Nectarine Chutney

Makes about 4 cups

When you think chutney, you think mango chutney, right? Yeah, me too. But then I was standing at the market in late summer, staring at a pile of nectarines from a nearby farm. I wondered, "Why not take spices from a culture on the other side of the world and pair it with a seasonal local fruit?" Nectarines and mangos share similarities in texture and sweetness, and this chutney proves it.

2 dried red chiles: 1 chopped, 1 kept whole

2 cinnamon sticks

2 cardamom pods, crushed

1 teaspoon cumin seeds

1 teaspoon coriander seeds

1 whole clove

1 cup water

½ cup cider vinegar

½ cup sugar

1 garlic clove, minced

2 teaspoons minced peeled fresh ginger

1½ teaspoons kosher salt

8 large firm nectarines, pitted and cut into ½-inch chunks (do not peel)

1 Combine the chiles, cinnamon sticks, cardamom pods, cumin seeds, coriander seeds, and clove on a piece of cheesecloth, and secure the bundle with kitchen twine. Place it in a large saucepan and add the water, vinegar, sugar, garlic, ginger, and salt. Bring to a boil, stirring to dissolve the sugar, and boil for 5 minutes.

2 Stir in the nectarines, cover, reduce the heat, and simmer for 20 minutes. The fruit should be soft but not mushy.

3 Remove from the heat and discard the spice sachet. Ladle into sterilized jars and jar properly or refrigerate for up to 3 months.

Serve with Curried Potato Samosas (page 165) or with any Indian meal. It's also nice with fried paneer (page 26).

. . . .

Carla's Tips

• Tart underripe nectarines make this a chunky savory chutney for main dishes; juicy ripe ones turn it into a smoother sweet jam.

. . . .

Peach Jalapeño Jam

Makes about 6 cups

Credit goes to Julia Phillips, my former catering sous chef, as the inspiration for this jam. The day she made it, she taught me that you don't have to be Southern to create something that tastes like the South. Julia's from Pennsylvania and she's always had a way with jams. One day, we got a load of juicy summer peaches in the catering kitchen. Julia simmered them with jalapeños to serve with chicken and waffles for a long-time client. Our client loved the jam so much, she wanted to buy jars of it! Yes, it's that good.

9½ cups large-diced peeled pitted ripe
    yellow peaches from 8 large
    (3¼ pounds)

1½ cups sugar

1 small jalapeño chile, stemmed, seeded,
    and minced

5 strips lemon zest, removed with a
    vegetable peeler

¼ cup fresh lemon juice

1 teaspoon kosher salt

1 In a large colander, toss the peaches and sugar until well mixed. Set over a large bowl and let stand for 30 minutes. Reserve the accumulated juices for anything you'd like: tea, dessert, cocktails.

2 In a large saucepan, bring the peaches, jalapeño, lemon zest and juice, and salt to a boil. Adjust the heat to a simmer and cook for 30 minutes.

3 Use a potato masher to lightly mash the fruit. Discard the lemon zest. Ladle the mixture into sterilized canning jars and jar properly or refrigerate for up to 3 months.

Carla's Tips

• You can easily peel ripe peaches with a serrated peeler. Or, to quickly and cleanly peel the peaches, lightly score an "x" on the stem end of each one. Drop the peaches into a pot of boiling water and let them bob around until the peel just starts to gape at the "x," 10 to 30 seconds, depending on ripeness. When they are cool enough to handle, peel off the skins.

• To seed a jalapeño chile, trim off the stem end. Sit the chile with the cut end down on a cutting board, and cut along the walls to remove the flesh in sections. The seeds attached to the ribs in the center will remain as a single unit.

• When I was developing this recipe, I found that marinating the peaches in sugar before cooking them gave the mix a much more complex savory flavor. If you prefer a traditional sweet jam, skip the first step and simmer the peaches with the sugar and remaining ingredients as directed in step 2.

• **Some Like It Hot:** For a spicy jam, keep the jalapeño seeds in and mince them with the chile.

Grains & Starches

I love connecting with people on an everyday level, so I often find myself tasting great grain dishes. Whenever I travel to other parts of the world, I find that grains and starches are the fuels that keep people going in their day-to-day lives. We're lucky enough in this country to usually enjoy them as side dishes, but the recipes below are so tasty, they can be much more than supporting actors on the plate. I like to make the most of humble ingredients like cornmeal, rice, and potatoes by using the right techniques to cook them properly. Once you've mastered that, you'll get a taste of the world in these easy sides.

. . . .

Creamy Cornmeal

Even though I didn't cook during my childhood in Nashville, I did know how to make grits: I just knew I had to stir and stir and stir. Cornmeal does this magical thing if you do that while it's simmering in liquid: It becomes light-as-air creamy. The more you stir, the lighter it will get. Neglect it a little and you'll end up with a heavier mix and little clumps. Neglect it a lot and you'll have sludge scorched on the bottom of your pan. The stirring can actually be therapeutic. You don't have to think about it—just get in the zone and keep going until the cornmeal is tender and creamy.

 SOUTHERN

Creamy Cheese Grits

Serves 8

I love grits. Period. I grew up loving them in the South, where they're a staple on all tables. Even the worst cooks in our family never made bad grits because we all know the secret: There's no such thing as quick grits. Cornmeal has to completely cook through to go from raw bitter gritty to smooth sweet creamy. Even if a package claims "1-minute cooking," the "quick grits" have to be stirred over heat for at least 15 minutes. Better yet, take the time to do them right: Start with stone-ground grits and stir for a good long time. Mascarpone may not be native to the South, but it makes my version extra decadent and creamy.

2¹/₂ cups whole milk

2¹/₂ cups Vegetable Stock (page 103) or store-bought unsalted vegetable broth, plus more if needed

Kosher salt

1¹/₂ cups white stone-ground grits

3 tablespoons unsalted butter, cut into pieces

¹/₂ cup mascarpone cheese

1 In a large saucepan, combine the milk and stock and season generously with salt. Whisk the grits into the cold liquid. Then continue whisking while bringing to a boil over medium heat. As soon as it comes to a boil, reduce the heat to maintain a light simmer.

2 Continue cooking, whisking very frequently, until the grits are soft and creamy and most of the liquid has been absorbed, about 40 minutes. If the mixture becomes dry before the grits soften, add more stock.

3 Stir in the butter and mascarpone until they melt and are fully incorporated into the grits. Season to taste with salt. Serve immediately.

• •

Carla's Tips

• Of course, you can use any cheese you like. Cheddar's a classic; goat cheese makes it tangy; Parmigiano-Reggiano, nice and salty. You can even leave out the cheese altogether for a pure creamy corn flavor.

• •

ITALIAN

Parmigiano-Reggiano Polenta

Serves 8

The difference between grits and polenta? The latter tends to cost more than the former in restaurants (though the rise of haute Southern cuisine is changing that . . .). Other than that, they're basically the same thing: cornmeal simmered low and slow until thick and creamy. When I first cooked and tasted polenta in culinary school, I definitely didn't make the connection. To me, grits were always white and often topped with shrimp. Polenta was thinner and yellow and I thought of it as a different animal. After years of making vats of both, I've come to realize how alike they are. You don't have to stir as religiously here because the cornmeal's cooked in water, so there's no risk of dairy scorching. But you still have to stir a lot! You don't want any lumps in your final dish.

7 cups water

Kosher salt

1¹/₂ cups stone-ground yellow cornmeal

4 tablespoons (¹/₂ stick) unsalted butter, cut into pieces

1¹/₂ cups freshly grated Parmigiano-Reggiano cheese, plus more for serving

Freshly ground black pepper

1 In a large saucepan, bring the water to a boil. Reduce the heat to maintain a gentle simmer and add 1 teaspoon salt. Add the cornmeal in a slow, steady stream while stirring continuously with a wooden spoon.

2 Reduce the heat to low, cover, and cook for 45 minutes, stirring and scraping the bottom of the pot every 5 minutes. When the polenta is really soft and smooth, it should look like thin mashed potatoes and have lost its raw cornmeal taste and gritty texture.

3 Add the butter, cheese, and a pinch each of salt and pepper, stirring until the butter melts. Serve immediately.

. . . .

Carla's Tips

• As soon as polenta starts to cool, it stiffens. If you know you're going to have leftovers, spread the extra warm, soft polenta in an even layer in a well-oiled rimmed pan. Cover and refrigerate until stiff. When you're ready to enjoy the leftovers, cut the cold polenta into small pieces and pan-fry or broil until golden brown, crisp, and warmed through.

. . . .

 JAMAICAN

Sweet Breakfast Porridge

Serves 6

Sweetened condensed milk is a staple in the Caribbean and so many other tropical regions where fresh milk spoils easily. I first learned this when I met Rhoda, a girl from Haiti, who happened to be on my post-college trip to Asia. She stirred that intensely sugary milk into everything from her breakfast cereal to her coffee. It works perfectly in this porridge, adding body and sweetness to the cornmeal-flour mix that tastes like a cross between grits and Cream of Wheat. I think the amount of sweetener here is plenty, but you can always add more to taste.

1 cup whole milk

4 cups water

1 teaspoon kosher salt

1 cup stone-ground yellow cornmeal

1 tablespoon all-purpose flour

3 tablespoons sweetened condensed milk

1 teaspoon ground cinnamon

1 teaspoon vanilla extract

Carla's Tips

• As with oatmeal, you can make a big batch of this on the weekend, and then refrigerate portions to zap in the microwave on busy weekday mornings.

1 In a large saucepan, combine the milk, water, and salt. Whisk the cornmeal, and then the flour, into the cold liquid; then continue whisking while bringing to a boil over medium heat. As soon as it comes to a boil, reduce the heat to maintain a light simmer. Whisk in the sweetened condensed milk, cinnamon, and vanilla.

2 Continue cooking, whisking frequently, until the porridge is soft and creamy, about 40 minutes. The porridge should have lost its raw cornmeal and flour taste. Serve immediately.

Rice

I love rice, **both brown** **and white varieties,** in all its forms. Different countries and regions specialize in different grains that range in texture from sticky and chewy to loose and firm depending on their length (long-, medium-, or short-grain) and starchiness. The only rule that applies to all rice: Be sure to rinse it well before using. Combine the grains with cold water in a large bowl and swish them around with your hands. Pour out the water and repeat until the water runs clear.

UNIVERSAL

Perfect Baked Rice

Serves 4

One of the first things I learned in culinary school was how to cook rice. I had thought it was a no-brainer. Then I learned how easily anyone can mess up something as simple as rice. After all, home cooks all around the world have rice cookers so they don't have to worry about the rice coming out right. My foolproof technique is just as good: The rice never burns, the water is absorbed evenly, and you can ignore it once it goes in the oven. Use this method with any variety, but it works best with standard, not specialty, grains.

1½ cups water or Chicken or Vegetable Stock (page 103) or store-bought unsalted broth

1 tablespoon butter or oil (optional)

1 cup rice, well rinsed and drained

1 Preheat the oven to 350°F.

2 In a large ovenproof saucepan with a lid, bring the water and butter, if using, to a boil over high heat. Stir in the rice, remove from the heat, cover, and pop into the oven.

3 Bake until the water is absorbed and the rice is perfectly tender, 17½ minutes. Really: 17½ exactly. I did this for years when I was catering and that was the magic number. Of course, ovens are different, so yours may take a little more or less time.

INDIA

Chitrana Peanut-Coconut Rice

Serves 8

Once I tasted this nutty, aromatic rice, I knew I wanted it in this book. As a professional chef, I can get any ingredients I want. For this rice, I used curry leaves and tamarind. Both can be hard to track down in regular supermarkets, so I replicated the flavor of traditional curry leaves with lemon zest and basil. And instead of tamarind, I use lemon juice and brown sugar. Of course the flavors aren't exactly the same, but they come pretty close and perfume the peanut-sesame-coconut combo nicely. What's really important, though, is that this dish is delicious!

2 cups basmati rice, rinsed

Kosher salt

1/4 cup roasted, salted peanuts

2 tablespoons white sesame seeds

2 tablespoons unsalted butter

1 garlic clove, minced

1/2 teaspoon yellow mustard seeds

1/2 teaspoon crushed red chile flakes

2 tablespoons flaked unsweetened coconut

1 tablespoon light or dark brown sugar

1/2 teaspoon ground turmeric

Grated zest and juice of 1 lemon

2 tablespoons torn fresh basil leaves

1 Bring a large saucepan of water to a boil. Add the rice and 1½ teaspoons salt. Boil, like pasta, until tender, about 10 minutes. Drain thoroughly and spread out on a large baking sheet to cool and dry.

2 Meanwhile, grind the peanuts and sesame seeds together in a spice grinder. Transfer to a small skillet and cook, stirring, over medium heat until fragrant and toasted, about 3 minutes. Transfer to a plate to cool.

3 In a large Dutch oven, melt the butter over medium-low heat and add the garlic. Cook, stirring, until fragrant, about 1 minute. Add the mustard seeds and chile flakes and cook for 30 seconds. Then stir in the coconut, brown sugar, turmeric, lemon zest, peanut-sesame blend, and rice. Continue stirring until the sugar dissolves and the mixture is heated through. Fold in the basil and lemon juice, and serve immediately.

. . . .

Carla's Tips

• This is a great use of leftover basmati rice. Start at step 2, and just throw in 4 cups cooked rice at the end and stir until heated through.

. . . .

Rice

I love rice, both brown and white varieties, in all its forms. Different countries and regions specialize in different grains that range in texture from sticky and chewy to loose and firm depending on their length (long-, medium-, or short-grain) and starchiness. The only rule that applies to all rice: Be sure to rinse it well before using. Combine the grains with cold water in a large bowl and swish them around with your hands. Pour out the water and repeat until the water runs clear.

UNIVERSAL

Perfect Baked Rice

Serves 4

One of the first things I learned in culinary school was how to cook rice. I had thought it was a no-brainer. Then I learned how easily anyone can mess up something as simple as rice. After all, home cooks all around the world have rice cookers so they don't have to worry about the rice coming out right. My foolproof technique is just as good: The rice never burns, the water is absorbed evenly, and you can ignore it once it goes in the oven. Use this method with any variety, but it works best with standard, not specialty, grains.

1½ cups water or Chicken or Vegetable Stock (page 103) or store-bought unsalted broth

1 tablespoon butter or oil (optional)

1 cup rice, well rinsed and drained

1 Preheat the oven to 350°F.

2 In a large ovenproof saucepan with a lid, bring the water and butter, if using, to a boil over high heat. Stir in the rice, remove from the heat, cover, and pop into the oven.

3 Bake until the water is absorbed and the rice is perfectly tender, 17½ minutes. Really: 17½ exactly. I did this for years when I was catering and that was the magic number. Of course, ovens are different, so yours may take a little more or less time.

PERSIAN

Jeweled Rice with Fruits and Nuts

Serves 8

This jeweled rice, javaher polow, *is usually reserved for weddings and other big celebrations. It's definitely a showstopper and feels—and tastes—very special. I learned the secrets to this dish over many years: First, my high school friend's family taught me about the crust; then, a family I cooked for as a private chef taught me to cover the lid with a tea towel to absorb excess moisture while the rice steams; finally, my friend Najmieh walked me through the rest of the steps. And there are a lot. Bits of dried fruit and seeds are mixed with sweetened carrot and orange rind strips, nuts, and warm spices, then layered with saffron-scented rice. Yes, it's a lot of work. And yes, it's totally worth it.*

1 orange

1 large carrot, peeled

1 cup plus ¼ teaspoon sugar

3 cups basmati rice

Kosher salt

4 tablespoons (½ stick) unsalted butter

1 medium yellow onion, very thinly sliced

1 teaspoon ground cardamom

1 teaspoon ground cinnamon

½ teaspoon ground cumin

½ teaspoon ground turmeric

½ cup slivered almonds

½ cup shelled pistachios

½ cup golden raisins

¾ cup pomegranate seeds

½ teaspoon saffron threads

¼ cup plain Greek yogurt

2 tablespoons canola oil

1. Remove the orange zest with a vegetable peeler. Very thinly slice each strip of zest crosswise. Place in a sieve and rinse under very hot water to remove any bitterness. Drain. Use the vegetable peeler to peel the carrot into long, thin ribbons. Very thinly slice the ribbons crosswise. Combine the 1 cup sugar, orange zest, and carrot ribbons with 1 cup water in a small saucepan. Bring to a boil, then reduce the heat and simmer for 10 minutes. Drain through a sieve placed over a bowl. Reserve the orange zest and carrot. Cover and refrigerate the simple syrup for another use.

2. Bring a large saucepan of water to a boil. Add the rice and 1 tablespoon salt. Boil, like pasta, until just tender on the outside but still crunchy in the center, about 6 minutes. Drain well and spread out on a large baking sheet to cool and dry.

3. Melt 2 tablespoons of the butter in a large saucepan over medium heat. Add the onion and ½ teaspoon salt. Cook, stirring frequently, until the onion is melted down to light golden tenderness, about 10 minutes. If the onion starts to get too dark, add a little water to the pan.

(continued on next page)

4 Add the cardamom, cinnamon, cumin, and turmeric and stir well for 1 minute. Add the almonds, pistachios, raisins, pomegranate seeds, and orange zest–carrot mixture. Stir for 2 minutes and then remove from the heat.

5 In a small bowl, grind the saffron with the remaining ¼ teaspoon sugar. Stir half of the saffron mixture and ½ cup of the cooked rice into the yogurt until well mixed. Stir the remaining saffron mixture into ½ cup water in a small bowl until the sugar dissolves.

6 In a large, wide nonstick or enameled cast-iron saucepan, heat the oil and remaining 2 tablespoons butter over medium-low heat, swirling to coat the bottom of the pan. Add the yogurt rice in a single, even layer. Cook, without touching it, until it sets, about 5 minutes. If it seems to be cooking too quickly, reduce the heat. You don't want the rice to burn.

7 Reduce the heat to low. Spoon one-third of the remaining rice over the yogurt layer, mounding it into a pyramid, and then add ½ cup of the fruit-nut mixture. Repeat the layering again. Use the handle of a wooden spoon to poke 4 holes in the rice without hitting the crust. Sprinkle the saffron water over the rice. Cover the pan's lid with a kitchen towel and set it over the rice tightly.

8 Cook until the rice is just tender throughout, about 15 minutes. Remove from the heat and let stand, covered, for 10 minutes. Spoon the rice onto a serving platter, and then use a spatula to place the tah dig, the golden crust, crunchy side up, on top.

• •

Carla's Tips

• Mulberries are the fruit traditionally used in this rice. If you can get your hands on some—fresh or dried—definitely use them here. I swapped in easy-to-find pomegranate seeds to try to capture mulberries' sweet-tartness.

• Use the leftover syrup in the Spiced Citrus Simple Syrup (page 190) to make Baklava (page 188) for dessert.

• •

Here are a just few specialty rices worth trying:

- America: Carolina: long, loose grains with a mild sweetness
- Italy: Arborio or Carnaroli: medium grains that should be cooked according to a good risotto recipe
- Spain: Bomba or Calasparra: highly absorbent grains ideal for paella
- India and the Middle East: Basmati: fragrant long grains that can be cooked like pasta
- Thailand and Southeast Asia: Jasmine: grains with a floral aroma
- Japan: Sushi: short and sticky grains that should be seasoned for sushi

The People in Your Neighborhood

There weren't a lot of different people in my Nashville neighborhood, so I was excited when a new girl moved nearby. She was Persian and her family was the most elegant I'd ever met. They invited me over for dinner one night and when they brought Persian rice with tah dig, a golden brown crust, to the table, I asked, "What's this rice cake?" I was blown away by how delicious it was. I'd never seen or tasted anything like it.

Since then, I've been on a quest to perfect tah dig. To crack the code on the crust, I went to my friend and Persian cooking expert Najmieh Batmanglij. Najmieh knows countless tah dig tricks, but the best is using a Persian rice cooker designed to create a foolproof crust. Until I buy one, I follow these simple steps:

- Go nonstick: Use a nonstick saucepan or an enameled cast-iron Dutch oven.

- Keep it low: The easiest way to mess up tah dig is to burn it. Keep the heat as low as possible so that the crust slowly turns golden.

- Scoop and scrape: My instinct is to flip the finished rice out of the pot onto a platter so that the tah dig ends up on top. That's going to leave you with a big mess.

- Instead, scoop out the rice on top, then use a flexible spatula to release the crust from the bottom and flip it upside down over the rice so that the crusty side is up.

INDIAN

Chitrana Peanut-Coconut Rice

Serves 8

Once I tasted this nutty, aromatic rice, I knew I wanted it in this book. As a professional chef, I can get any ingredients I want. For this rice, I used curry leaves and tamarind. Both can be hard to track down in regular supermarkets, so I replicated the flavor of traditional curry leaves with lemon zest and basil. And instead of tamarind, I use lemon juice and brown sugar. Of course the flavors aren't exactly the same, but they come pretty close and perfume the peanut-sesame-coconut combo nicely. What's really important, though, is that this dish is delicious!

2 cups basmati rice, rinsed

Kosher salt

¼ cup roasted, salted peanuts

2 tablespoons white sesame seeds

2 tablespoons unsalted butter

1 garlic clove, minced

½ teaspoon yellow mustard seeds

½ teaspoon crushed red chile flakes

2 tablespoons flaked unsweetened coconut

1 tablespoon light or dark brown sugar

½ teaspoon ground turmeric

Grated zest and juice of 1 lemon

2 tablespoons torn fresh basil leaves

1 Bring a large saucepan of water to a boil. Add the rice and 1½ teaspoons salt. Boil, like pasta, until tender, about 10 minutes. Drain thoroughly and spread out on a large baking sheet to cool and dry.

2 Meanwhile, grind the peanuts and sesame seeds together in a spice grinder. Transfer to a small skillet and cook, stirring, over medium heat until fragrant and toasted, about 3 minutes. Transfer to a plate to cool.

3 In a large Dutch oven, melt the butter over medium-low heat and add the garlic. Cook, stirring, until fragrant, about 1 minute. Add the mustard seeds and chile flakes and cook for 30 seconds. Then stir in the coconut, brown sugar, turmeric, lemon zest, peanut-sesame blend, and rice. Continue stirring until the sugar dissolves and the mixture is heated through. Fold in the basil and lemon juice, and serve immediately.

• •

Carla's Tips

• This is a great use of leftover basmati rice. Start at step 2, and just throw in 4 cups cooked rice at the end and stir until heated through.

• •

 ALL-AMERICAN

Rice Pilaf

Serves 4

This is one of basic things that I learned and never forgot. I never even had a recipe for it. I took my favorite herb, thyme, and added butter and onion to bring a fragrant richness to rice. The first time I did it, I had an aha! moment when I couldn't find a lid for my cooking dish. Foil works even better because it traps in the moisture and flavors. This is a great technique for passive cooking for a crowd because you don't have to worry about direct heat potentially burning your rice. Plus, the principle behind the dish is a blank palette for you to try other seasonings. The flavors here go with just about any American or Western European dish, but you can use the same technique and play with any herb-spice combination you want.

2 tablespoons unsalted butter

1/2 cup diced yellow onion

1 teaspoon fresh thyme leaves, chopped

1 teaspoon kosher salt

1 cup white rice

1 1/2 cups water or Chicken or Vegetable Stock (page 103) or store-bought unsalted broth

1 Preheat the oven to 350°F. In a large ovenproof saucepan with a lid, melt the butter over medium heat. Add the onion and cook, stirring occasionally, until golden brown and tender, about 5 minutes.

2 Stir in the thyme and salt, then stir in the rice. Cook, stirring, until the rice is toasted, about 2 minutes. Add the water and bring to a boil. Cover, transfer to the oven, and bake until the rice is tender and has absorbed all of the liquid, about 17 minutes. Fluff with a fork and serve.

Carla's Tips

• If you don't want to turn on your oven, you can cook the rice on the stove. After bringing the liquid to a boil, cover the pan, adjust the heat to maintain a bare simmer, and cook until the rice has absorbed all the liquid, about 20 minutes.

Potatoes

I grew up on spuds and consider mashed potatoes one of the best foods ever. Even though that's my favorite way of enjoying potatoes, I also love 'em fried, roasted, sautéed, even simply boiled. Its subtle flavor is what makes the potato so versatile. For a long time, it seemed you could get only one or, at best, two types of potatoes in the supermarket. Now, you can find a whole range of varieties! Some are sweet and buttery, others nutty and fluffy.

Even though there are a ton of options out there, you can think of potatoes in two basic categories: waxy and floury. Waxy potatoes, such as red, Yukon gold, new, and fingerlings, have thinner skins, more sugar, and less starch than floury potatoes. Their dense, sweet flesh is great boiled, roasted, fried, and stewed. Floury potatoes, such as all-purpose, russets, and Idahoes, have tougher brown skins and more starch. Their mealy, nutty flesh absorbs liquid readily, making them ideal for mashed potatoes and fries.

 ALL-AMERICAN

Roasted Fingerling Potatoes

Serves 4

Simple, simple, simple—that's what I really love in the kitchen. And this couldn't be easier. Just toss potatoes with oil and roast. I don't add the thyme and seasonings until they're almost done so that the herbs stay fresh. The salt also keeps its crunch that way, so you get that French-fry-like yummi- ness when you first bite down into a piping-hot potato, then sink your teeth into the refined creamy sweetness of fingerlings.

1 pound fingerling potatoes, scrubbed

2 tablespoons extra virgin olive oil

1 teaspoon fresh thyme leaves

1/2 teaspoon kosher salt

1/2 teaspoon freshly ground black pepper

1 Preheat the oven to 400°F. On a rimmed baking sheet, toss the potatoes with the oil until well coated. Roast for 30 minutes or until tender.

2 Toss the thyme, salt, and pepper with the po- tatoes until evenly coated. Return the pan to the oven and roast for 5 minutes longer. Serve hot.

· ·

Carla's Tips

• Buy a variety of fingerlings to make this dish pretty. Some even have cool pink stripes in the center!

· ·

Curried Potatoes and Peas

Serves 4

My husband, Matthew, makes a red curry potato dish and I adapted his recipe when I was catering. Potatoes can take a lot of spice, so I decided to go with a bold yellow curry. It's important to start with potatoes that can hold their shape when they cook and then to cut them pretty big. Otherwise, they'll turn to mush. Even though I usually make this as a filling for Samosas (page 165), it's also fantastic as a side dish.

6 medium Yukon gold potatoes, peeled

Kosher salt

1 tablespoon unsalted butter

1 tablespoon canola oil

1½ cups diced yellow onions

½ cup diced carrots

2 teaspoons curry powder

½ cup frozen peas, thawed

1 cup Vegetable Stock (page 103) or store-bought unsalted vegetable broth

1 Place the potatoes in a large pot and add enough cold water to cover by 2 inches. Generously salt the water and bring to a boil over high heat. Reduce the heat to a simmer and cook until just tender, about 20 minutes.

2 Drain well, then spread out in a single layer on a cutting board. When cool enough to handle, cut the potatoes into ½-inch chunks.

3 Heat the butter and oil in a large skillet over medium heat until the butter melts. Add the onions and 1 teaspoon salt. Cook, stirring occasionally, until the onions have browned, about 7 minutes. Stir in the carrots and 2 tablespoons water and cook, stirring and scraping the pan, until the water evaporates.

4 Stir in the curry powder until well mixed. Then add the potatoes, peas, and stock. Cook, stirring to mix, for 2 minutes. Remove from the heat and serve hot (or cool completely to use as filling for samosas).

GERMAN

Double-Mustard Potato Salad

Serves 8

In my world, there's Southern-style mayo-drenched potato salad and then there's everything else. I've always called that "everything else" category of uncreamy salads "German." Can't say why, I just do. Maybe it's simply because I like true German potato salads, served all warm and mustardy. Too much mustard can take any dish over the edge. Surprisingly, mustard seeds alone are mild. What they offer is a fantastic pop! when you bite into them. Here they're brightened up by the Dijon in the dressing. When I made this, I debated whether or not the salad really needed the bacon. (It's not traditional—it's just delicious.) I thought it was tasty without the bacon, but it was way better with just that little extra savory, crunchy kick.

1½ pounds small red potatoes, scrubbed

Kosher salt

1 tablespoon cider vinegar

2 teaspoons Dijon mustard

¼ cup extra virgin olive oil

1 teaspoon yellow mustard seeds

2 tablespoons minced fresh flat-leaf parsley leaves

1 tablespoon minced fresh chives

3 strips bacon, cooked and crumbled

1 Place the potatoes in a large pot and add enough cold water to cover by 2 inches. Generously salt the water and bring to a boil over high heat. Reduce the heat to a simmer and cook until just tender, about 20 minutes.

2 Drain well, and then spread the potatoes out in a single layer on a cutting board to cool slightly.

3 Meanwhile, in a large bowl, whisk the vinegar, Dijon, and ¼ teaspoon salt until smooth. Continue whisking while adding the oil in a slow, steady stream until emulsified.

4 When they are cool enough to handle, cut the potatoes into quarters. Add the warm potatoes, mustard seeds, parsley, and chives to the dressing and fold gently until well mixed. Top with the bacon and serve.

. . . .

Carla's Tips

• Use a sharp knife to cut the cooked potatoes, and rinse and wipe the blade between cuts if it gets too sticky. That way, you can keep the pretty skin intact.

. . . .

Seafood

I know how it feels to be scared of cooking fish. I grew up in landlocked Nashville and the only fresh fish dish I ever knew was the fried catfish served at church suppers. We never made it at home and fish simply wasn't part of our diet. That's why I've focused on two foolproof types of fish dishes here: stews and salmon. For the former, all you have to do is throw in the fish at the end to poach in the flavorful stew base you've created. For the latter, just do everything you can to avoid overcooking this super-easy-to-find tasty fish.

In all of the recipes in this chapter, I want you to take the fish off the heat when it's just opaque throughout. The fish will continue to cook as it rests and will get to perfectly done this way. If a recipe calls for fish stock, you can try to buy some from a fish shop or other good market. You can also substitute bottled clam juice for the stock. If you do that, season carefully as clam juice can be quite salty.

Stews

When I was creating these recipes, I asked the nice fish guy at my favorite neighborhood market for the freshest catch he had. He gave me a variety of fish and they were all so fresh, they smelled nice and sweet and not at all fishy. When you make these stews, you should do the same. It's much more important to buy the freshest fish than to get a specific type that's stinky. If you can't find the types specified here, you can use other types as long as they're thick and meaty. Thin, flaky fillets will fall apart too easily if simmered in a stew, and even less delicate hearty fillets break apart when cooked. That's why I have you keep the fish in big chunks before they go into the simmering stews. They'll become bite-size pieces once you start scooping the stew out into bowls for serving.

Cod and Potato Chowder

Serves 12

This started as a spin on my classic oyster stew for a big catering job. The flavors work well with mild, flaky cod, which poaches gently in the soup at the end. It was such a hit at that event that I've been doing it ever since. Bacon and clam juice bring strong savory notes to this dish, so season carefully throughout to avoid making the stew too salty.

4 strips bacon

1 cup finely diced yellow onion

1 cup finely diced celery

1 cup finely diced fennel bulb

4 sprigs fresh thyme

Zest of 1 lemon, removed with a vegetable peeler

Kosher salt and freshly ground white pepper

1 quart fish stock or clam juice

1½ cups finely diced peeled Yukon gold potatoes

1 cup finely diced peeled celery root

1 quart whole milk

2 fresh or dried bay leaves

3 tablespoons unsalted butter

¾ cup all-purpose flour

¼ teaspoon cayenne pepper

1 pound skinless cod fillets, cut into 3-inch chunks

¼ cup heavy cream

¼ cup chopped fresh flat-leaf parsley leaves

3 sprigs fresh tarragon, chopped

1 In a large saucepan, cook the bacon over medium heat, turning occasionally, until browned and crisp, about 10 minutes. Transfer to paper towels to drain. Crumble and reserve.

2 To the fat in the pan, add the onion, celery, and fennel. Cook, stirring occasionally, until the onion is translucent, about 5 minutes. Add the thyme and lemon zest and cook, stirring, for 3 minutes. Add a pinch each of salt and white pepper.

3 Meanwhile, in another large saucepan, bring the fish stock to a boil. Reduce the heat to medium, add the potatoes and celery root, and cook until just tender, about 10 minutes.

4 Strain the fish stock through a sieve into the pan containing the vegetables, reserving the potatoes and celery root. Stir the milk and bay leaves into the pan. Adjust the heat to maintain a steady simmer.

5 In a large skillet, melt the butter over medium heat and then whisk in the flour. Continue whisking while slowly adding 1½ cups of the liquid from the saucepan. When fully incorporated, stir the flour mixture into the saucepan. Stir in the cayenne. Bring to a simmer and cook, stirring occasionally, until thickened, about 5 minutes. Season to taste with salt and white pepper.

6 Carefully add the cod to the saucepan, submerging the fish. Adjust the heat to maintain a bare simmer. Cook until the fish is just opaque throughout, about 5 minutes. Stir in the cream, parsley, and tarragon, and season to taste. Remove and discard the bay leaves, thyme sprigs, and lemon zest. Top with the bacon, potato, and celery root, and serve.

• •

Carla's Tips

• My refined cheffy way of making this dish is to separately sauté the fennel and celery in a little oil until just crisp and then stir them in at the end. You can do that too if you'd like.

• •

Coconut Fish Stew

Serves 8

Usually we try to pick fish bones out. In this Brazilian dish, I want to keep the bones in. They add great depth and you do discard them before serving the stew. (Word to the wise: The tastiest fish is right on the bones. I like to suck the meat off the bones that are meant to go in the garbage. It's a treat for me and a way to avoid wasting food!) Because the shrimp and fish cook quickly at the end, you need to develop the stew's deep flavors first, and the bones add a lot to that.

1½ pounds large shrimp, peeled and deveined

1 whole red snapper (1²/₃ pounds), scaled, gutted, and filleted, bones and head reserved

1/3 cup fresh lime juice, plus lime wedges for serving

5 garlic cloves, minced

3 tablespoons extra virgin olive oil

Kosher salt and freshly ground black pepper

2 medium yellow onions, diced

1 medium red bell pepper, stemmed, seeded, and cut into 1/4-inch dice

1 medium green bell pepper, stemmed, seeded, and cut into 1/4-inch dice

1/2 teaspoon crushed red chile flakes

2 large ripe tomatoes, cored and cut into 1/4-inch dice

1 cup fish stock or clam juice

1 cup Vegetable Stock (page 103) or store-bought unsalted vegetable broth

1 fresh or dried bay leaf

1 cup coconut milk

1 tablespoon finely chopped fresh cilantro leaves

1 In a large bowl, combine the shrimp, snapper fillets, lime juice, two-thirds of the garlic, 1 tablespoon of the oil, ½ teaspoon salt, and ¼ teaspoon pepper. Cover and refrigerate.

2 Heat the remaining 2 tablespoons oil in a large Dutch oven or flameproof casserole over medium-high heat. Add the onions and 1 teaspoon salt and cook, stirring occasionally, until the onions are just translucent, about 2 minutes. Add the bell peppers and cook, stirring occasionally, for 2 minutes. Add the chile flakes and remaining garlic and cook, stirring, for 1 minute.

3 Add the tomatoes, fish stock, vegetable stock, bay leaf, and the fish head and bones, and bring to a boil. Reduce the heat and simmer for 10 minutes.

4 Stir in the coconut milk and cilantro and simmer for 5 minutes. Add the shrimp and fish fillets with their marinade. Cover, reduce the heat to low, and cook until the fish and shrimp are just opaque throughout, about 5 minutes. Don't let the mixture boil at this point—the lime juice could cause the coconut milk to break. Remove and discard the fish head and bones and bay leaf. Season to taste and serve with lime wedges.

(continued on next page)

Carla's Tips

• Get your fishmonger to prepare your fish for you if you don't want to do it yourself. Often, they'll just sell the fillets (already removed from the fish). In that case, ask for the bones they keep stashed in the back.

• Marinate the shrimp and fish only as long as it takes to prep and simmer the soup. Any longer and their delicate flesh will start to break down.

Cilantro Fish Stew

Serves 6

Some dishes in this book can't be attributed to any one culture. This isn't exactly Thai or Vietnamese—it borrows flavors from all over Southeast Asia. What I love about similar soups I've tasted I've combined here, namely keeping whole slices of ginger and lemongrass in the stew. I had debated whether I should fish them out before serving, but decided to stick with tradition and keep them in. Of course you don't eat them, but you smell their yummy aromas while you're sipping the stew. That scent, mingled with the fragrance of fresh herbs, adds an amazing dimension to the light, clean flavors here.

1½ cups fish stock or clam juice

3 cups water

One 3-inch piece fresh ginger, peeled and thinly sliced at an angle

2 stalks lemongrass, white and pale yellow parts only, trimmed, smashed, and cut into 2-inch pieces

1 serrano chile, cut into very thin rounds, with the seeds

2 garlic cloves, very thinly sliced

7 scallions (green onions), trimmed, whites and greens thinly sliced separately

Kosher salt

¾ cup coconut milk

3 small carrots, peeled, cut in half lengthwise and very thinly sliced at an angle

4 large white button mushrooms, trimmed and very thinly sliced

2 teaspoons Asian fish sauce

1¼ pounds skinless halibut or other meaty white fish, cut into 3-inch chunks

1 cup sliced fresh cilantro leaves

1 tablespoon sliced fresh mint leaves

1. Bring the fish stock, water, ginger, lemongrass, chile, garlic, scallion whites, and ½ teaspoon salt to a boil in a large saucepan. Reduce the heat and simmer for 5 minutes. Then stir in the coconut milk and simmer for 2 minutes.

2. Add the carrots, mushrooms, and fish sauce and simmer until the carrots are just tender, about 3 minutes.

3. Add the halibut, reduce the heat to low, and cook until the fish is barely opaque throughout, about 4 minutes. Add the cilantro, mint, and scallion greens and cook for 1 minute. Season to taste, and serve.

. . . .

Carla's Tips

• **Some Like It Hot:** Stir some sambal oelek or sriracha into the stew just before serving.

. . . .

Tomato-Pepper Mahi-Mahi Stew

Serves 8

When I was living in London, a friend from Ghana taught me that all of her native dishes start with onions, peppers, and tomatoes. And they call everything "stew," even if the dish doesn't seem that stewy. This one does, with meaty thyme-marinated mahi-mahi in a thick sweet and spicy tomato mix.

2 pounds skinless mahi-mahi or other hearty white fish, cut into 3-inch chunks

2 tablespoons plus 1 teaspoon canola oil

1 teaspoon chopped fresh thyme leaves, plus 2 sprigs fresh thyme

Kosher salt and freshly ground black pepper

1 medium yellow onion, diced

1 medium red bell pepper, stemmed, seeded, and cut into 1/2-inch dice

1 medium green bell pepper, stemmed, seeded, and cut into 1/2-inch dice

1 jalapeño chile, stemmed and minced, with seeds

3 garlic cloves, minced

2 tablespoons tomato paste

One 14.5-ounce can diced fire-roasted tomatoes

2 cups Vegetable Stock (page 103) or store-bought unsalted vegetable broth

1 fresh or dried bay leaf

1 In a large bowl, combine the fish, 1 teaspoon oil, the chopped thyme, 1 teaspoon salt, and 1/4 teaspoon pepper.

2 In a large saucepan, heat the remaining 2 tablespoons oil over medium-high heat. Add the onion, bell peppers, jalapeño, and 1 teaspoon salt. Cook, stirring occasionally, until just starting to soften, about 3 minutes. Add the garlic and cook, stirring, for 1 minute. Add the tomato paste and cook, stirring, for 2 minutes.

3 Add the tomatoes with their juices, stock, bay leaf, and thyme sprigs. Bring to boil, then reduce the heat to medium and simmer, uncovered, for 20 minutes.

4 Carefully add the fish and submerge it in the liquid. Cover, reduce the heat to medium-low, and cook until the fish is just opaque throughout, about 8 minutes. Discard the bay leaf and thyme sprigs. Season to taste and serve immediately.

Broiled Salmon

Broiling is my tried-and-true quick cooking technique for salmon. It gets it nice and crisp on the outside without the risk of the fish sticking to a pan or grill grate. The inside stays nice and juicy under the direct heat, too. Plus, working in the broiler keeps my stovetop spotless.

 ALL-AMERICAN

Dijon Tarragon Salmon

Serves 4

Sometimes it's the dead-simple dishes that trip me up. I made this a million times to get it right. First, I had way too much mustard, so I cut its spiciness with creamy mayo. Then I threw in some tarragon for a classic French combo . . . but then I wanted more tarragon to get just the right hint of licorice in the mix. I know I keep encouraging you to experiment with my recipes in the kitchen—and you should—but you can also follow this one step-by-step to get a perfect superfast weeknight dinner the first time around. Now that I messed up my fish, you don't have to.

3 tablespoons Dijon mustard

3 tablespoons minced fresh tarragon leaves

1½ tablespoons mayonnaise

Four 6-ounce center-cut salmon fillets

1 Set the broiler rack 6 inches from the heat source. Preheat the broiler to high. Line a rimmed baking sheet with foil.

2 In a small bowl, stir together the Dijon, tarragon, and mayonnaise. Place the salmon on the baking sheet and slather the tops and sides with the mixture.

3 Broil until opaque on top but still slightly translucent in the middle, about 8 minutes.

· ·

Carla's Tips

• Lining the pan with foil means super easy cleanup!

· ·

Salmon Teriyaki

Serves 4

You want easy? I got your easy. The simple sauce simmers while the fish broils, then glazes the salmon at the end. But I learned the hard way that sometimes you can't just wing it when creating a dish. Teriyaki is a balance between salty, sweet, and tanginess. I fell in love with it on a recent trip to Japan. When I got home, I went full strength on all flavors on my first attempt. I thought the rich salmon could take the intensity, but it's still delicate. When I used too much soy, I got the salt first, then the fish. I perfected the sauce so that you'd first taste the fish and then get the teriyaki. Once I found that balance, I kept trying versions of the sauce to find just the right substitute for mirin, a sweet wine traditionally used in teriyaki. If you have some, use the same amount in place of the brown sugar here. Otherwise, this mix tastes as great as any and works well with grilled chicken and steak too.

¼ cup packed light or dark brown sugar

¼ cup water

2 tablespoons soy sauce

½ teaspoon rice vinegar

One 1-inch piece fresh ginger, peeled and sliced

1 garlic clove, smashed

Four 6-ounce center-cut salmon fillets

1. Set the broiler rack 6 inches from the heat source. Preheat the broiler to high. Line a rimmed baking sheet with foil.

2. In a small saucepan, bring the brown sugar, water, soy sauce, vinegar, ginger, and garlic to a boil, stirring to dissolve the sugar. Reduce the heat to maintain a steady simmer and cook for 10 minutes, until the sauce has thickened. Discard the ginger and garlic.

3. Place the salmon on the baking sheet and broil until just opaque on the surface, about 5 minutes. Remove from the broiler, and spoon a thin layer of the sauce all over the fillets. Return to the broiler and cook until just opaque on top but still translucent in the center, about 3 minutes. The sauce should be browned and bubbling.

4. Transfer to serving plates and spoon the remaining sauce all over.

Serve with short-grain white rice.

Chicken

Undoubtedly the most popular protein for simple weeknight dinners, chicken should be celebrated for how yummy it really is. I find a chicken dinner—regardless of its seasonings—the most comforting meal. The one condition I have for a proper chicken dish: Start with good chicken. Look for birds that are sustainably free-range, fed an organic feed, and raised without antibiotics. Ideally, get a local bird that's really fresh. Once you've done that, the rest is easy.

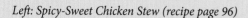

Skillet Stews

When you hear the word "stew," you think of hours of simmering. But chicken cooks far faster than that, and when you put the bird in a wide, shallow pan, it goes even faster. I approached these skillet stews as weeknight meals because that's how easy they are. But with all their homey warmth, they taste like a Sunday supper.

Left: Spicy-Sweet Chicken Stew (recipe page 96)

 WEST AFRICAN

Spicy-Sweet Chicken Stew

Serves 4

My ancestors are from Nigeria and my brother-in-law is from Liberia. If there's one key lesson I've taken from him and my extended family, it's that the triumvirate of tomatoes, green peppers, and onions is the foundation of West African cooking. In this quick stew, I start with a whole chicken, including the bones, which add such big flavor that you can simply use water to create a tasty sauce. If you want, you can use chicken stock instead for a super-rich stew. I love the sweetness of tomatoes, banana, and mango with the fruity heat and spice of habanero chile in this hearty one-dish dinner.

1 habanero chile

One 28-ounce can whole San Marzano
   tomatoes

Extra virgin olive oil, for frying

One 3-pound chicken, cut into 8 pieces
   (2 wings, 2 breasts, 2 drumsticks, 2
   thighs)

Kosher salt

1 medium yellow onion, finely chopped

1 medium green bell pepper, stemmed,
   seeded, and finely chopped

2 garlic cloves, finely chopped

Freshly ground black pepper

2 fresh or dried bay leaves

$1/2$ teaspoon dried thyme

$3^1/_2$ cups water

1 ripe banana, peeled

1 ripe mango, peeled and pitted

1 Cut a small slit in the chile. This will prevent the seeds from spilling into the stew and making it incredibly hot. Set it aside. Empty the can of tomatoes into a large bowl. Gently squeeze the tomatoes with your hands to crush them into large chunks. Set the tomatoes aside.

2 Fill a large Dutch oven or flameproof casserole with oil to a depth of ⅛ inch, and heat it over medium-high heat until hot but not smoking. The oil should dimple and have wavy lines. Season the chicken generously with salt and add it to the hot oil, skin side down, spacing the pieces apart. Don't crowd the pan; work in batches if you have to.

3 Reduce the heat to medium. When the skin is dark golden brown, turn the pieces over. Continue cooking until the bottom is dark golden brown. Transfer the chicken to a plate.

4 Add the onion, bell pepper, garlic, ¼ teaspoon salt, and a pinch of black pepper to the skillet. Cook, stirring frequently, until the onion is nice and soft, about 7 minutes.

5 Stir in the bay leaves, thyme, and habanero chile. Cook, stirring, for 2 minutes. Stir in the water and tomatoes. Heat to a boil, then adjust the heat to maintain a steady simmer.

6 Nestle the chicken pieces in the sauce, skin side up, and add any accumulated juices from the plate. The sauce shouldn't cover the skin. Partially cover the pan and simmer until the chicken is cooked through, about 30 minutes. If some pieces are done before others, remove them first and place them on a plate.

7 While the chicken cooks, puree the banana and mango in a food processor or blender until smooth. Stir the mixture into the sauce when the chicken is done.

8 Remove and discard the chile and bay leaves from the stew, and serve hot.

Serve with Perfect Baked Rice (page 71)—lots of it if you make the stew extra spicy.

• •

Carla's Tips

• This is definitely one of those stews that gets better as it sits. The heat and sweet flavors really develop and balance each other.

• **Some Like It Hot:** Cut a larger slit in the chile or, if you can take it, cut the whole thing in half to make this dish spicier.

• •

FRENCH

Chicken in Dijon Cream

Serves 4

I learned this dish early on in cooking school and it's still one of my go-to quick and easy meals. When I first visited France, I didn't taste anything like this. But, I'll be honest, I didn't taste much. I was so into the lardon *salads that I didn't try many other things. Since then, I've had fuller French dining experiences. Now, when I dig into this creamy sauce, with mustard and wine perfectly balancing the richness, I feel like I'm in Paris again.*

4 boneless, skinless chicken breast halves (2 pounds total)

Kosher salt

1 tablespoon extra virgin olive oil, plus more if needed

1/2 tablespoon unsalted butter, plus more if needed

1/2 small yellow onion, minced

1/4 cup dry white wine

1 cup Chicken Stock (page 103) or store-bought unsalted chicken broth

1 tablespoon Dijon mustard

1/4 cup heavy cream

1 1/2 teaspoons chopped fresh thyme leaves

1 1/2 teaspoons chopped fresh tarragon leaves

1 On a large cutting board, place the chicken between sheets of wax paper. Pound with a meat mallet, rolling pin, or heavy skillet until the meat is an even 1/2 inch in thickness. Season the chicken generously with salt.

2 Heat a large, heavy skillet over medium-high heat until hot. Coat with the oil, then add the butter. When the butter is foamy but not brown, add half the chicken, smooth side down. Cook until browned, about 3 minutes. Then carefully flip the chicken over and cook until nicely browned but not cooked through, about 2 minutes longer. Transfer to a plate. Repeat with the remaining chicken, reheating the pan and replenishing the oil and butter if necessary.

3 Add the onion to the skillet and cook, stirring and scraping up the browned bits and bobs, until it is just soft, about 1 minute. Add the wine and cook until reduced by half, then add the stock. Simmer for 1 minute.

4 Whisk in the Dijon and cook, stirring, until the mustard is well incorporated, about 1 minute. Stir in the cream and a pinch of salt, and bring to a boil. Reduce the heat to maintain a steady simmer, and then slide in the chicken and the accumulated juices. Partially cover and simmer until the chicken is cooked through, about 2 minutes. Stir in the thyme and tarragon, and serve hot.

Serve with a good crusty baguette and a crisp green salad.

• •

Chicken with Milk Gravy

Serves 4

Grandma Thelma used to make this for quick, casual dinners. She'd start by plucking off the extra fat on the chicken (and, of course, saving it for cooking later). Then she'd fry the flour-coated meat in her cast-iron skillet before smothering it with milk gravy. I don't coat my chicken in flour before frying because it makes the skin all flabby. I get the skin nice and crisp and keep it away from the gravy until serving time. That way, I get crunchy chicken and creamy sauce in each bite.

2 tablespoons all-purpose flour

Pinch of garlic powder

Pinch of dried thyme

Pinch of cayenne pepper

**Kosher salt and freshly ground black
    pepper**

Extra virgin olive oil, for frying

**8 bone-in, skin-on chicken thighs
    (2 pounds total), excess fat and excess
    skin removed**

1 medium yellow onion, finely chopped

2 garlic cloves, finely chopped

**1³/₄ cups Chicken Stock (page 103) or
    store-bought unsalted chicken broth**

¹/₄ cup whole milk

1 In a small bowl, combine the flour, garlic powder, thyme, cayenne, and a pinch each of salt and pepper. Set aside.

2 Fill a large cast-iron skillet with oil to a depth of ⅛ inch, and heat it over medium-high heat until hot but not smoking. The oil should dimple and have wavy lines. Season the chicken generously with salt and add it to the hot oil, skin side down, spacing the pieces apart. Don't crowd the pan; work in batches if you have to.

3 Reduce the heat to medium. When the skin is dark golden brown, turn the pieces over. Continue cooking until the bottom is dark golden brown. Transfer the chicken to a plate.

4 Add the onion and ¼ teaspoon salt to the skillet. Cook, stirring, for 1 minute. Then stir in the garlic and cook, stirring frequently, until the onion is nice and soft, about 7 minutes.

5 Whisk in the spiced flour and cook, whisking continuously, for 1 minute. Continue whisking rapidly and add the chicken stock in a slow, steady stream. Turn the heat to low to maintain a steady simmer. Nestle the chicken pieces in the gravy, skin side up, and add any accumulated juices from the plate. The sauce shouldn't cover the skin. Partially cover the skillet and simmer until the chicken is cooked through, about 20 minutes.

6 Transfer the chicken to serving dishes. Whisk the milk into the gravy and cook, whisking continuously, just until heated through. Season to taste with salt and pepper. Spoon around the chicken, and serve immediately.

**Serve over Perfect Baked Rice (page 71) or
mashed potatoes with a nice green salad.**

Chicken with Sour Cream and Paprika

Serves 4

This dish is where this whole book started. I asked myself, "How can I take a comforting dish I love, like fried chicken in milk gravy, and change it? How can I change a chicken dish to represent another flavor?" I have a limited knowledge of Hungarian food, but I know sour cream and paprika are mainstays in the cuisine. And I knew, from a catering disaster years ago, the secret to adding sour cream to a savory heated sauce: You have to do it over very low heat. When you do, you get a beautiful, incomparable silkiness. I especially love the finish on this dish, the little tingle of heat on my lips tempered by the rich cream sauce.

Extra virgin olive oil, for frying

8 bone-in, skin-on chicken thighs (2 pounds total), excess fat and excess skin removed

Kosher salt

1 medium yellow onion, finely chopped

2 serrano chiles, stemmed, seeded, and thinly sliced

2 garlic cloves, finely chopped

½ teaspoon sweet paprika

Pinch of cayenne pepper

1 cup Chicken Stock (page 103) or store-bought unsalted chicken broth

⅓ cup sour cream

2 tablespoons chopped fresh flat-leaf parsley leaves

1 Fill a large, heavy skillet with oil to a depth of ⅛ inch, and heat it over medium-high heat until hot but not smoking. The oil should dimple and have wavy lines. Season the chicken generously with salt and add it to the hot oil, skin side down, spacing the pieces apart. Don't crowd the pan; work in batches if you have to.

2 Reduce the heat to medium. When the skin is dark golden brown, turn the pieces over. Continue cooking until the bottom is dark golden brown. Transfer the chicken to a plate.

3 Add the onion, chiles, garlic, and ¼ teaspoon salt to the skillet. Cook, stirring frequently, until the onion is nice and soft, about 7 minutes.

4 Stir in the paprika and cayenne and cook for 1 minute. Stir in the chicken stock, bring to a boil, and then reduce the heat to maintain a steady simmer. Nestle the chicken pieces in the sauce, skin side up, and add any accumulated juices from the plate. The sauce shouldn't cover the skin. Partially cover the skillet and simmer until the chicken is cooked through, about 20 minutes.

5 Transfer the chicken to serving dishes. Reduce the heat to low so that the sauce no longer simmers. Whisk the sour cream into the gravy until just heated through. Don't let the sauce come to a boil or it'll break. Spoon the sauce around the chicken and top with the parsley. Serve immediately.

Serve with Roasted Fingerling Potatoes (page 79) or boiled new potatoes.

Carla's Tips

• **Swap Out:** Hot paprika is a fragrant, complex Hungarian spice. I love it, but it can be hard to track down in stores here. I've combined sweet paprika, cayenne pepper, and hot serrano chiles to mimic that flavor. If you can find hot Hungarian paprika, definitely use it in place of the sweet paprika and drop the cayenne. But keep the chiles; they add a unique fresh, bright heat.

Soups

Talk about soul food! Chicken in broth—that's all you need to feel good inside. I know I'm not the only one who craves this when I'm feeling a little under the weather. You'll feel even better if you start with homemade stock and take care to not overcook the chicken. Even though the chicken is in liquid, it can still get overcooked and taste dry. Be sure to take your soup off the heat as soon as the chicken loses its pinkness throughout.

Stock 101

I often use my pressure cooker when making stock to get more intense flavors in less time. Use the quantities here and cook for half the time, carefully following the manufacturer's instructions for releasing the pressure before opening the pot.

I like to keep a little fat in the stock for richness, but if you want to get rid of it, refrigerate the stock overnight. By the next day, the fat will have risen to the top and solidified. You can scrape and dump it (or save it for cooking!).

I don't season my stocks with salt; I season the dishes the stock is used in. This helps me avoid having unintentionally over-seasoned dishes. Stock freezes beautifully. I like to freeze it in half-pint and pint-size heavy plastic deli containers so I know how much I've got in each container. I stick a piece of masking or painter's tape on the container and label and date it so I know how old it is.

Chicken Stock

Makes about 12 cups

Honestly, I'll buy stock when I don't have time to make it. But when I do, I'm always moved to mmmmmm by what a difference homemade makes. Its pure, clean flavors really come through in any dish. The seasonings here work with dishes from wherever in the world, but if you want to tailor the stock to a particular cuisine, check out the International Spice Chart (page xvi) and toss in the right aromatics, herbs, and spices. Stocks are meant to be adjusted to your taste, so the ingredients below are just a jumping-off point for you.

8 large carrots, peeled and chopped

4 large celery ribs, chopped

2 medium yellow onions, chopped

2 pounds chicken wings, backs, necks, or a combination

3 fresh or dried bay leaves

1 tablespoon black peppercorns

1 tablespoon dried thyme leaves

1 In a 12- to 14-quart stockpot, combine all of the ingredients. Add cold water to cover by 2 inches and bring to a boil over high heat, skimming the foam and scum from the surface. Then cover partially, reduce the heat, and simmer for 2 hours.

2 Strain through a fine-mesh sieve and discard the solids. The stock can be refrigerated in airtight containers for up to 3 days or frozen for up to 3 months.

Vegetable Stock

Omit the chicken, double the vegetables, and proceed as above. You can also add other vegetable trimmings you may have handy.

INDIAN

Spicy Tomato Chicken Soup
Serves 6

Imagine a cross between chicken curry and tomato stew: now you have this stick-to-your-ribs soup. I layer the seasonings here, from the chicken marinade to the sautéed vegetables to the flour for thickening. Building the spices brings out the complexity of the whole and keeps the flavors from getting muddy. Even with those separate steps, this soup comes together quickly.

2 whole bone-in chicken breasts, skin discarded, bones cut out and reserved, meat cut into 2-inch chunks

2 serrano chiles, cut in half lengthwise and thinly sliced, seeded if desired

2 garlic cloves, minced

3 sprigs fresh cilantro, plus fresh cilantro leaves for garnish

2 fresh or dried bay leaves

Kosher salt

2 tablespoons canola oil

1 large yellow onion, diced

1/2 teaspoon ground green curry leaves

1/2 teaspoon garam masala

1 large tomato, diced

3 cups Chicken Stock (page 103) or store-bought unsalted chicken broth

3 cups water

1 teaspoon cumin seeds

2 tablespoons all-purpose flour

1/2 teaspoon ground turmeric

1 In a large bowl, combine the chicken meat and bones, chiles, garlic, cilantro sprigs, bay leaves, and 1 teaspoon salt. Toss until well mixed.

2 Heat 1 tablespoon of the oil in a large Dutch oven or flameproof casserole over medium heat. Add the onion and 1/2 teaspoon salt and cook, stirring occasionally, until the onion is translucent and tender, about 5 minutes. Add the curry and garam masala and cook, stirring, for 1 minute. Add the tomato and cook for 1 minute, stirring.

3 Add the chicken stock, water, and the chicken with its seasonings. Raise the heat to high. As soon as the liquid comes to a boil, lower the heat immediately. (This step makes the difference between rubbery, horrible chicken and silky, tender chicken.) Adjust the heat to maintain a bare simmer, skimming any foam and scum from the surface.

4 Cover the pan and poach the chicken for 15 minutes. Remove and discard the chicken bones, bay leaves, and cilantro sprigs.

5 In a small skillet, heat the remaining 1 tablespoon oil over medium heat. Add the cumin seeds and whisk for 1 minute. Add the flour and turmeric and whisk for 1 minute. Then whisk in 1/4 cup of the hot chicken liquid and cook for 1 minute, whisking. Stir the mixture into the soup. Cook until thickened, about 5 minutes, then season with salt to taste. Garnish with cilantro leaves and serve.

Serve with Chitrana Peanut-Coconut Rice (page 76), Palak Paneer (page 26), or naan.
• •

Souse: Chicken Soup with Lime

Serves 6

For years, I spent every winter in the Bahamas as a private chef. But I never managed to go out to eat because I worked 'round the clock. When I had the chance to return to the island for Top Chef: All-Stars, *I made a point of dining out. My friend Tiffany Derry and I hit this spot that specialized in souse, a traditional lime-y chicken soup. It was sooooo good! The hint of allspice and the richness of homemade stock made the dish super tasty. With each sip of this soup, I feel like I'm back on the beach.*

1 teaspoon freshly grated lime zest

1 teaspoon dried thyme

¼ teaspoon freshly ground white pepper

¼ teaspoon cayenne pepper

Kosher salt

½ cup plus 3 tablespoons fresh lime juice

4 chicken legs, thighs and drumsticks separated

2 tablespoons canola oil

1 large green bell pepper, stemmed, seeded, and cut into ½-inch chunks

1 large yellow onion, cut into ½-inch chunks

1½ pounds baby red potatoes, scrubbed and cut into ½-inch chunks

5 small carrots, peeled and cut into ½-inch chunks

4 garlic cloves, sliced

1 tablespoon allspice berries, coarsely ground

2 fresh or dried bay leaves

½ teaspoon crushed red chile flakes

5 cups Chicken Stock (page 103) or store-bought unsalted chicken broth, plus more if needed

1 In a large bowl, rub the lime zest, thyme, white pepper, cayenne, and 1 teaspoon salt with the chicken. Massage the 3 tablespoons lime juice into the meat. Cover and refrigerate for 1 hour.

2 Heat the oil in a large Dutch oven or flame-proof casserole over high heat. Add the bell pepper, onion, and 1 teaspoon salt. Cook, stirring frequently, until browned, about 5 minutes. Reduce the heat to medium and add the potatoes, carrots, garlic, allspice, bay leaves, and chile flakes. Stir well, then nestle the chicken pieces in the mixture. Add enough stock to just cover the chicken.

3 Bring the mixture to a boil over high heat, then reduce the heat to maintain a steady simmer. Stir in the remaining ½ cup lime juice, cover, and simmer for 30 minutes or until the chicken is cooked through. Remove and discard the bay leaves, season to taste with salt, and serve.

Serve with Creamy Cheese Grits (page 68) or johnnycakes.

• •

Carla's Tips

• **Some Like It Hot:** Add another ½ teaspoon crushed red chile flakes.

• •

ISRAELI

Chicken Soup with Chicken Liver Dumplings

Serves 8

Keep the soup itself light and pure so the rich dumplings shine. Leave out the dumplings and you have the framework for a basic quick chicken soup.

2 medium carrots, peeled and cut in half

2 celery ribs, cut in half

1 medium yellow onion, cut in half

2 whole bone-in, skin-on chicken breasts

1 fresh or dried bay leaf

8 cups Chicken Stock (page 103) or store-bought unsalted chicken broth

Chicken Liver Dumplings (recipe follows)

Kosher salt

1 tablespoon chopped fresh cilantro leaves

1 In a large saucepan or Dutch oven, bring the carrots, celery, onion, chicken, bay leaf, and stock to a boil. Reduce the heat and simmer until the chicken is just cooked through, about 15 minutes. Discard the carrots, celery, onion, and bay leaf. Transfer the chicken to a plate, leaving the stock simmering in the pot. When the chicken is cool enough to handle, remove and discard the skin and bones. Pull the meat against the grain into large slivers.

2 Add the dumplings to the simmering stock and cook, stirring gently, until cooked through, about 5 minutes. Add the chicken meat and simmer until heated through. Season to taste with salt. Stir in the cilantro and serve hot.

Chicken Liver Dumplings

Makes about 2 dozen

Joan Nathan is the queen of Jewish cooking. I've been lucky to get to know her personally, but I knew of her work long before. She told me about kubbeh, *Israeli (by way of Iraq) semolina and meat dumplings simmered in chicken soup. To make the filling extra rich, I've added chicken livers and spices. Make your own dumpling wrappers with semolina; the mixture is the easiest I've ever handled.*

Ras El Hanout

½ teaspoon coriander seeds, ground

½ teaspoon cumin seeds, ground

½ teaspoon freshly grated nutmeg

½ teaspoon ground turmeric

½ teaspoon sweet smoked paprika

¼ teaspoon cardamom seeds, ground

¼ teaspoon allspice berries, ground

¼ teaspoon freshly ground cinnamon

¼ teaspoon cayenne pepper

⅛ teaspoon freshly ground black pepper

Dumplings

4 ounces ground beef chuck (80% lean)

Kosher salt

¼ cup finely diced yellow onion

1 garlic clove, minced

4 ounces chicken livers, veins removed, chopped

1 teaspoon finely chopped fresh cilantro leaves

1 cup fine semolina flour, or more if needed

½ cup cold water

Canola oil, for shaping dumplings

1 To make the ras el hanout: In a small bowl, mix all the spices together. The blend will keep in an airtight container at room temperature for up to 2 weeks.

2 To make the dumplings: Heat a large skillet over medium-high heat until very hot. Add the beef and ½ teaspoon salt and cook, stirring to break the meat into tiny bits, until it is just browned, about 1 minute. Push the beef to one side of the pan, and add the onion and garlic to the other side of the pan. Cook in the beef fat, stirring until just translucent, about 1 minute. Push to the side with the beef, and add the chicken livers and ¼ teaspoon salt to the other side. Cook, stirring gently, until just browned, about 10 seconds. Stir into the beef and onion and remove from the heat. The liver should still be pinkish. Stir in the *ras el-hanout* and cilantro.

3 In a large bowl, stir the flour and ¼ teaspoon salt to combine. Stir in the water and continue stirring until the dough forms a ball. It shouldn't stick to your fingers. If it does, add a little more semolina. Roll the dough into a 1-inch-diameter log, and then cut the log crosswise into ½-inch pieces.

4 Lightly oil your hands. Roll 1 piece of the dough into a ball, and then press it to form a ⅛-inch-thick round. Make an indentation in the center with your thumb and put 1 teaspoon of the filling in the indentation. Fold the dough in half to enclose the filling, and press the edges to seal into a half-moon. Repeat with the remaining dough and filling.

5 Cook in the chicken soup as directed or simply boil in salted water until cooked through, about 5 minutes.

 SOUTHERN

Chicken and Dumplings

Serves 6

Now these are some tasty dumplings. All I wanted to do in this recipe was to make dumplings the way my great-aunt Minnie used to. She had the magic touch that made the lightest, fluffiest dumplings ever. Because she visited us only once a year from her home in Michigan, we got to have this dish only once a year. Aunt Minnie was so famous for her dumplings—even in our town—that Granny, her sister, wouldn't even attempt to make a batch! We all just waited patiently for her to come and cook them for us. There's no secret formula, though. I think it just takes practice to get it right, to handle the dough as quickly and gently as possible in order to keep the dumplings light as air.

Chicken Soup

3 tablespoons canola oil

1 large yellow onion, diced

Kosher salt

3 sprigs fresh thyme

4 medium carrots, peeled and cut into
  ¹/₂-inch pieces

2 celery ribs, cut into ¹/₂-inch slices at
  an angle

Freshly ground black pepper

1 tablespoon all-purpose flour

4 whole chicken legs, drumsticks and
  thighs separated (or 4 each chicken
  drumsticks and thighs)

3 cups Chicken Stock (page 103) or store-
  bought unsalted chicken broth

Dumplings

1 cup all-purpose flour

1¹/₂ teaspoons baking powder

¹/₂ teaspoon table salt

3 tablespoons cold unsalted butter, cut
  into pieces

¹/₂ cup buttermilk

1 To make the soup: In a large Dutch oven, heat 2 tablespoons of the oil over medium-high heat. Add the onion and ½ teaspoon salt and cook, stirring occasionally, until just tender, about 2 minutes. Add 2 of the thyme sprigs, stir well, and continue cooking until the onion is translucent, about 1 minute. Add the carrots, celery, and ½ teaspoon pepper. Cook just until the celery is bright green, about 4 minutes. Transfer to a large bowl. Remove and discard the thyme sprigs.

2 Add the remaining 1 tablespoon oil to the Dutch oven. Sprinkle the flour and ½ teaspoon each salt and pepper all over the chicken. Add to the pan in a single layer, skin side down. Cook until golden brown on both sides, about 10 minutes. Transfer to a plate, and carefully drain the fat from the pan.

3 Add ½ cup of the stock to the pan and cook, stirring and scraping the browned bits from the bottom of the pan. Return the chicken to the pan, skin side up, and add 1½ cups stock and the remaining thyme sprig. Bring to a boil, then cover partially and reduce the heat to maintain a steady simmer. Simmer until the chicken is cooked through, about 30 minutes. Remove and discard the thyme sprig. Add the remaining 1 cup stock and the vegetables. Bring to a boil, then adjust the heat to maintain a steady simmer.

4 While the chicken simmers, make the dumplings: In a large bowl, mix the flour, baking powder, and salt. Then cut in the butter, using your fingertips, until coarse crumbs form. Add the buttermilk and stir just until the mixture is combined.

5 Take two spoons and dip them in the simmering soup. Use one spoon to scoop the dumpling dough and the other to push the dough into the soup. Repeat scooping and dropping the dough, using the spoons to push the dumplings apart as they puff. Cover the pot and simmer just until the dumplings are cooked through, about 5 minutes. Serve hot.

Chicken Pasta Soup

Serves 6

My sister, Kim, really enjoyed this soup when I brought some to her. I think it's because it tastes a lot like the classic American chicken soup we grew up on, but with a zing from the fresh pesto. There's basil in the soup, too, and the double dose of freshness tastes great all year round.

Pesto

1 garlic clove, peeled

¼ teaspoon kosher salt

1 cup packed fresh basil leaves

1 tablespoon fresh oregano leaves

¼ cup finely grated Parmigiano-Reggiano cheese

¼ cup extra virgin olive oil

Soup

2 tablespoons extra virgin olive oil

3 medium carrots, peeled and diced

1 celery rib, diced

1 small yellow onion, diced

1 garlic clove, minced

1 sprig fresh basil

Kosher salt

One 3-pound chicken, cut into 4 pieces (2 whole legs, 1 whole breast with wings attached, back), rinsed and patted dry

Freshly ground black pepper

4 cups Chicken Stock (page 103) or store-bought unsalted chicken broth

1 cup tiny round pasta, such as ditalini

Freshly grated Parmigiano-Reggiano cheese, for serving

1 To make the pesto: In a food processor, pulse the garlic and salt until finely chopped. Add the basil and oregano and pulse until finely chopped. Pulse in the cheese until well mixed. With the machine running, add the oil in a slow, steady stream. Reserve for serving (or refrigerate for up to 3 days or freeze for up to 3 months).

2 To make the soup: Heat 1 tablespoon of the oil in a large, heavy saucepan or Dutch oven over medium heat. Add the carrots, celery, onion, garlic, basil, and 1 teaspoon salt. Cook, stirring occasionally, until the vegetables are just tender, about 7 minutes. Transfer to a bowl.

3 Season the chicken with ½ teaspoon salt and ¼ teaspoon pepper. Heat the remaining 1 tablespoon oil in the same saucepan until hot but not smoking. The oil should dimple and have wavy lines. Add the chicken to the hot oil, skin side down, spacing the pieces apart. Don't crowd the pan; work in batches if you have to. Cook, turning once, until golden brown, about 6 minutes.

4 Add the stock and bring to a boil. Then reduce the heat and simmer until the chicken is cooked through, about 20 minutes. Transfer the chicken to a plate, leaving the stock simmering in the pan. When the chicken is cool enough to handle, discard the skin and bones. Pull the meat against the grain into large slivers.

5 While preparing the chicken, stir the pasta into the simmering stock and cook until al dente.

6 Return the chicken and vegetables to the pan and cook until just heated through. Stir in the pesto and season to taste with salt. Top with Parmigiano-Reggiano, and serve hot.

Fried

In my first cookbook, I gave you my recipe for traditional Southern fried chicken. As much as I love that straightforward classic, the two super seasoned recipes here are totally worth trying. The first is also from my hometown, but a far cry from the usual—it's for you hotheads out there. And the second is from the other side of the globe, bursting with all the flavors of Southeast Asia.

Fried chicken isn't nearly as scary or as hard as some people make it out to be. Sure, you see chicken going into vats of oil at restaurants, but that's not how you do it at home. I skillet-fry my chicken so it doesn't require a lot of oil and cooks quickly and evenly.

 SOUTHERN

Hot Fried Chicken
Serves 4

This is a Nashville delicacy. I'm proud to say that you can't find it outside my hometown—at least not the real thing—unless you make it at home. For years, I've been talkin' about doing it and now I finally have. I was so happy with my version that I went straight to Prince's in Nashville on my next trip home to see how mine stacked up with one of the most famous chicken shacks in town. I gotta say, mine can hold its own. If you like hot food and fried chicken, you'll love this dish.

Hot Brine

1 quart water

¼ cup habanero hot sauce or another really hot hot sauce

¼ cup kosher salt

¼ cup sugar

8 boneless, skin-on chicken thighs

Fried Chicken

¼ cup canola oil, plus more for frying

1 tablespoon cayenne pepper

½ teaspoon sweet paprika

¼ teaspoon garlic powder

½ teaspoon sugar

Kosher salt

2 cups all-purpose flour

Freshly ground black pepper

1 To brine the chicken: In a large bowl, whisk the water, hot sauce, salt, and sugar until the sugar dissolves. Submerge the chicken in the liquid and refrigerate for at least 1 hour and up to 6 hours.

2 To prepare the fried chicken: Heat the ¼ cup oil in a small saucepan over medium heat until shimmering. Add the cayenne, paprika, garlic powder, sugar, and 1 teaspoon salt. Cook, stirring, until fragrant, about 30 seconds. Transfer to a small bowl and reserve.

3 In a large resealable plastic bag or a paper bag, combine the flour with ½ teaspoon salt and 1 teaspoon black pepper. Add the chicken in batches and shake well until all the pieces are evenly coated.

4 Add enough oil to a cast-iron or other heavy skillet to reach ½ inch up the sides. Heat the oil over medium heat until it reaches 365°F. The oil's ready when a little flour dropped in bubbles and sizzles steadily.

5 Remove the chicken from the flour, shaking off any excess. Carefully place a few pieces of the chicken in the oil, skin side down. You don't want to crowd the pan. Keep adjusting the heat to keep a steady sizzle and to maintain 365°F. Cook until browned on the bottom, about 3 minutes, then carefully turn each piece over. Cook until browned on the bottom, about 3 minutes. Then continue cooking and turning to evenly brown until cooked through, about 10 minutes total. Crumple up some paper towels and drain the chicken on them.

6 Repeat with the remaining chicken, replenishing and reheating the oil between batches.

7 Transfer the chicken to a serving dish and drizzle with the reserved spice oil. Serve hot.

• •

Carla's Tips

• The cut of chicken here isn't commonly sold in markets, but it works best for this dish. Keeping the chicken boneless helps it cook through before the skin starts to burn, but it stays juicy because it's thigh meat. Your best bet is to buy bone-in, skin-on chicken thighs, then carefully cut the bones out. You can use the bones for Chicken Stock (page 103).

• •

THAI

Lemongrass-Ginger Fried Chicken

Serves 12

I love the clean flavors here. You can use this savory marinade and roast or grill the chicken instead of frying it. I'm partial to the frying, though, especially using this technique of lightly coating with cornstarch first. It'll get you a shatteringly crisp, thin skin. I couldn't settle on any one cut of chicken here because I like wings and Matthew prefers thighs; just be sure to stick with dark meat.

2 stalks lemongrass, white and pale yellow parts only, smashed and sliced

One 3-inch piece fresh ginger, peeled and chopped

1 teaspoon crushed red chile flakes

1/2 cup chopped fresh cilantro leaves

2 scallions (green onions), trimmed and thinly sliced

1 tablespoon dried shrimp (optional)

1 tablespoon light or dark brown sugar

1/4 cup fresh lime juice

2 tablespoons fish sauce

1 tablespoon soy sauce

3 pounds chicken thighs, wings, or drumsticks

Canola oil, for frying

1/2 cup cornstarch

Kosher salt

Hot sauce, for serving (optional)

1 In a food processor, pulse the lemongrass, ginger, chile, cilantro, scallions, shrimp, if using, and sugar until finely chopped. With the machine running, add the lime juice, fish sauce, and soy sauce. Transfer to a gallon-size, resealable plastic bag. Add the chicken and massage the marinade into the meat. Refrigerate for at least 1 hour and up to 4 hours.

2 Add enough oil to a cast-iron or other heavy skillet to reach 1/2 inch up the sides. Heat over medium heat until it reaches 365°F, when a little cornstarch dropped in bubbles and sizzles steadily.

3 Remove the chicken from the marinade, wiping off excess solids. Arrange in a single layer on a rimmed baking sheet. Place the cornstarch in a fine-mesh sieve and dust both sides of the chicken with the cornstarch.

4 Carefully place a few pieces of the chicken in the hot oil, skin side down. You don't want to crowd the pan. Keep adjusting the heat to keep a steady sizzle and to maintain 365°F. Cook until browned on the bottom, about 3 minutes, then carefully turn each piece over. Cook until browned on the bottom, about 3 minutes. Then continue cooking and turning to evenly brown until cooked through, about 10 minutes total. Crumple up some paper towels and drain the chicken on them.

5 Repeat with the remaining chicken, replenishing and reheating the oil between batches. Sprinkle with a little salt and serve hot, with hot sauce, if desired.

Chicken 'n Rice

Rice is like a sponge; it soaks up the liquid it's cooking in. That's why I love cooking it in chicken stock that also contains some chicken pieces. The combination adds such depth to the rice. Of course, fragrant aromatics help too. Even though both of the recipes here have Latin influences and start with the same aromatic base of sofrito, they showcase different ways to use the same flavors.

 LATIN

Arroz con Pollo

Serves 6

When Rosie Perez came to The Chew *as a guest, I got to make this dish with her. In her native Puerto Rico, the dish isn't about heat, and her family's version doesn't use bell peppers or chiles. But I want spice in my rice, so I went ahead and made it hot. Well, Rosie and I had to agree to disagree on this one, but we both gobbled down each other's takes on the same dish. And that's the thing with arroz con pollo: There are as many versions as there are cooks making it all over the world. Start with my base recipe here, then adjust the seasonings to create your own version.*

Sofrito

½ medium yellow onion, chopped

½ cubanelle pepper, stemmed, seeded, and chopped

½ medium red bell pepper, stemmed, seeded, and chopped

½ habanero chile, stemmed, seeded, and chopped

2 plum tomatoes, cored and chopped

½ head garlic, cloves peeled and chopped

½ bunch fresh cilantro, chopped

Arroz con Pollo

One 3½- to 4-pound chicken, cut into 8 pieces (2 wings, 2 breasts, 2 drumsticks, 2 thighs), rinsed and patted dry

Kosher salt and freshly ground black pepper

1 tablespoon canola oil

3½ cups white rice

1 teaspoon ground turmeric

3 cups Chicken Stock (page 103) or store-bought unsalted chicken broth

1 To make the sofrito: Combine all the ingredients in a food processor and pulse until very finely chopped. Use immediately or refrigerate in an airtight container for up to 3 days (but note that the raw onion and garlic may stink up your fridge).

2 To make the arroz con pollo: Season the chicken with 1 teaspoon salt and ½ teaspoon pepper. Heat the oil in a large heavy saucepan or Dutch oven over high heat. Add the chicken to the hot oil, skin side down. Don't crowd the pan; work in batches if you have to. Cook, turning once, until browned, about 10 minutes. Transfer to a plate.

3 Add the sofrito to the pan. Watch out! It'll smoke and may make you cough. Cook, stirring and scraping, until the raw edge mellows, about 5 minutes. Add the rice and turmeric. Cook, stirring, until the rice is toasted, about 3 minutes.

4 Add the stock and bring to a boil. Boil for 3 minutes, then season with salt to taste. Nestle the chicken pieces in the mixture and return to a boil. Then cover, reduce the heat to low, and simmer until the rice is tender and the chicken is cooked through, about 25 minutes. Serve hot.

Serve with Tangy Hot Cabbage Slaw (page 14).

. . . .

Carla's Tips

• You can also add chopped olives and/or diced carrots to the mix when you add the stock. If you want peas and/or corn, scatter them over the rice 5 minutes before it's done cooking.

. . . .

My Culinary Heritage

My family has been in America for generations. I grew up hearing stories of my great-grandparents' lives as slaves, my grandparents' struggles in the South, my parents' participation in the sit-ins. They've paved the way for me and fed me well along the way.

Southern soul food has always been a part of me. I knew its West African origins and the flavors that define it. What I didn't know, I learned from Jessica Harris, an amazing cookbook author who brilliantly tracked the African diaspora in *High on the Hog: A Culinary Journey from Africa to America.*

Her book, and my own life experiences, made me recognize the importance of passing on my culinary heritage to future generations. After Granny celebrated her ninety-second birthday, she grew too tired to continue cooking. Shortly after that, she passed on. As the passionate (and professional) cook in the family, I realized that I had to carry the torch.

Since Granny's death, I've been teaching her dishes to my mom, who never learned them from Granny, my brother-in-law, who's added his family's recipes to our collection, and my niece, who's in her first post-college kitchen. When they master a dish, they feel confident enough to try another and to add their own twists on tradition.

Last Thanksgiving, I didn't cook a thing. Though I've cooked the whole feast in years past, I simply handed everyone my first cookbook and told them to do whatever they wanted. It was amazing to have Granny's whole spread—and then some—on the table and to see how each family member tinkered with the recipes. That's what it's all about, really: keeping a taste of the past while creating new ones for the future.

AFRICAN

Jollof: Pepper and Chicken Rice

Serves 4

Even though this dish is part of my heritage, I first tried it as an adult. My brother-in-law invited my family over to his family's place for dinner. They're from Liberia, where they regularly cooked this dish at home. I was so fascinated by the red rice and the chicken cut up through the bones; I had never had rice like that before. It was so sticky and yummy and oily! I began searching out jollof rice after that and have tried countless versions from different West African countries. The version here is a combination of my favorites, made quick enough for weeknights with boneless meat.

1½ cups water or Chicken or Vegetable Stock (page 103) or store-bought unsalted broth

2 tablespoons tomato paste

2 tablespoons extra virgin olive oil

1 pound boneless, skinless chicken thighs or goat meat, cut into small chunks

Kosher salt

½ cup diced yellow onion

1 cup diced green bell pepper

1 tablespoon chopped garlic

1 teaspoon fresh thyme leaves, chopped

Pinch of cayenne pepper

1 cup white rice

1 Preheat the oven to 350°F. In a bowl or measuring cup, whisk together the water and tomato paste until smooth; reserve.

2 In a deep, wide ovenproof skillet with a lid, heat the oil over medium-high heat. Generously season the chicken with salt, then add to the hot oil. Cook, turning the pieces occasionally, until browned, about 5 minutes.

3 Add the onion, bell pepper, and garlic. Cook, stirring occasionally, until the vegetables are golden brown and tender, about 5 minutes.

4 Stir in the thyme, cayenne, and ½ teaspoon salt, and then stir in the rice. Cook, stirring, until the rice is toasted, about 2 minutes. Add the tomato liquid and bring to a boil. Cover, transfer to the oven, and bake until the rice is tender and has absorbed all of the liquid, about 17 minutes. (You can also leave the saucepan on the stove. Cover the skillet, adjust the heat to maintain a bare simmer, and cook until the rice has absorbed all the liquid, about 20 minutes.) Serve hot.

Carla's Tips

- **Some Like It Hot:** Throw in a bigger pinch of cayenne. If you want a huge amount of heat, add a Scotch bonnet pepper.

- **Love 'Em Leftovers:** Already grilled, roasted, or sautéed chicken or goat—or heck, any rich cooked meat—will work here. Just heat it with the sautéed onions, being careful to not overcook the meat.

Paella with Chicken, Chorizo, Mussels, and Shrimp

Serves 6

Think of this as a chicken dish that contains seafood, not as a seafood dish. The shrimp and mussels bring a sea-saltiness, but it's really about the chicken juices running into the rice and making this one-pan meal super satisfying. On my first attempt, I found it tricky to get the seafood cooked but not overcooked while cooking the rice to a perfect al dente chewiness. I discovered that the secret is to add a blast of heat at the very end of cooking. Not only does it finish the seafood, it also adds a rich toastiness to the rice.

4 tablespoons extra virgin olive oil

4 links (12 ounces) fresh chorizo, removed from casing and cut into 1-inch chunks

One 3^1/$_2$ to 4-pound chicken, cut into 8 pieces (2 wings, 2 breasts, 2 drumsticks, 2 thighs), rinsed and patted dry

Kosher salt

1 medium yellow onion, finely diced

^{1}/$_2$ recipe (about 1^1/$_2$ cups) Sofrito (page 116)

3 cups white rice, preferably bomba or cebolla

1 teaspoon sweet paprika

^{1}/$_2$ teaspoon dried oregano

^{1}/$_2$ teaspoon light or dark brown sugar

^{1}/$_2$ teaspoon saffron threads, mashed in 1 teaspoon water

4 cups Chicken Stock (page 103) or store-bought unsalted chicken broth

1 pound large shrimp, shelled and deveined

1 pound mussels, beards removed, scrubbed

Finely chopped fresh flat-leaf parsley leaves, for garnish

Lemon wedges, for serving

1 Heat 1 tablespoon of the oil in a deep, wide skillet over high heat. Add the chorizo chunks in a single layer. Cook, stirring to break the chunks up a little, until browned, about 4 minutes. Transfer to a plate.

2 Add 2 tablespoons oil to the pan. Season the chicken with 1 teaspoon salt and add to the pan, skin side down. Don't crowd the pan; work in batches if you have to, adding the remaining tablespoon of oil if needed. Cook, turning once, until browned, about 10 minutes. Transfer to another plate.

(continued on next page)

3 Reduce the heat to medium and add the onion and ½ teaspoon salt to the pan. Cook, stirring, until browned, about 2 minutes. Then add the sofrito. Watch out! It'll smoke and make you cough. Cook, stirring and scraping, until it is browned and nearly dry, about 10 minutes.

4 Add the rice, paprika, oregano, brown sugar, and saffron. Cook, stirring, until the rice is toasted, about 1 minute. Add the stock and ½ teaspoon salt, and bring to a simmer. Stir in the chorizo, then nestle the chicken pieces, skin side up, in the mixture. Return to a simmer, cover, reduce the heat to medium-low, and cook for 10 minutes.

5 Arrange the shrimp and mussels around the chicken, and cover the pan. Cook for 7 minutes, then raise the heat to high and cook for another 3 minutes. The shrimp should be opaque throughout and the mussels open. Garnish with parsley and serve with lemon wedges.

Carla's Tips

• Bomba and cebolla are medium-grain rices traditionally used in paella. They're especially absorbent, making them ideal for this dish, and are easy to find in specialty shops or online.

• **Swap Out:** Saffron can be pricey, so you can use a teaspoon of turmeric instead.

Lost in Translation

My first trip abroad was a high school Spanish class field trip. Mrs. Lolita, our favorite teacher, took us on a tour of Europe, which included an extended stay in Spain. I have two distinct memories of my time there.

The first involved a boy. I have no idea who he was or how he came to our group or why he was wearing a big sweater when it was so hot out. I guess he was just a local kid interested in us Americans. When I saw him approaching, I was excited to practice my Spanish. He opened with the reasonable, *"Cuantos años tienes?"* All he wanted to know was how old I was, but I blanked. I couldn't remember for the life of me how to say fifteen, so I kept repeating, *"Diez y cinco, diez y cinco!"* He looked at me as if to ask, "What?!" and walked away.

The second memory is much happier. We didn't get to choose where we ate, but our teacher selected some fantastic spots. One night, we all crammed into a tiny restaurant for dinner and were presented with a huge flat skillet of food to share. Mrs. Lolita elegantly swept her long brown hair behind her shoulders and explained that it was *paella,* arguably the national dish of Spain. For the first time in my life, I tasted perfectly cooked seafood. But it was the yellow rice that really got me. It was so chicken-y and delicious.

I forgot about that dinner until I was cooking professionally decades later. I've since eaten countless versions of paella, but that first one, shared with Mrs. Lolita and my high school buddies, remains, in my food memory, the best paella I've ever had.

Meat

Grill, roast, sear, sauté, braise: meat cooking techniques are nearly identical everywhere. The fun thing about meat is that you see it in these same forms, but with so many different flavors, all around the world. The seasonings change, and I'm always excited to try new spice and herb combos. I've taken a few of my meat standards and applied global tastes to them here. The most important thing is to buy sustainably raised meat that hasn't been treated with any antibiotics. I know it's tough to pay a bit more for meat; that's why I tend to eat it less frequently instead. When I do, it tastes like a real treat.

Burgers

Maybe they're not called burgers in other countries, but they're essentially the same thing: ground meat patted together, then cooked until browned. Plain, pure meat's tasty, but other cultures throw in spices that make these combos crazy good. I'm all about the fixins' and buns, but you can always ditch 'em and do these as meatballs.

Left: All-American Burgers 101 (recipe page 126)

 ALL-AMERICAN

Burgers 101

Serves as many as you want

One night last summer, my husband, Matthew, and I were craving burgers. Rather than go out for them, we decided to make them at home. Oh, man! Were they good! They hit the spot—and we didn't even fire up the grill. I realized that night that there's no real recipe for great burgers—only techniques that you have to follow to achieve burger perfection. Here's how it's done:

• Start with high-quality beef chuck that's 80% lean from local farmers or a good market. If you have a meat grinder, grind a chuck steak fresh. Otherwise, ask the butcher to do it for you.

• While you're at the market, pick up lettuce with crunch, like romaine, a firm onion, and a nice fat ripe tomato that's still firm enough to slice. Get good bread, too. I like the nutty earthiness of multigrain buns. Pop over to the deli section for thick squares of aged cheddar. Stock up on dill pickles, too. You can cut 'em at home yourself or buy the crinkle-cut pickle chips. If you're out of mayo and mustard, get those, also.

• Since this is a once-in-a-while treat, do ½ pound raw meat per patty. You don't want a wimpy burger. Gently pat the meat into a perfectly flat 1½-inch-thick round disk that's ½-inch wider than the bun. Don't overpack the meat; handle it as gently as possible. With your knuckle, dimple the center. Give the meat a shower of kosher salt and a sprinkle of pepper.

• If you have a stove hood, turn it on high. Otherwise, open a window. Heat a cast-iron skillet over medium-high heat until it's good and hot. Add a patty or two, no more. If you crowd the meat, it'll start to steam and get gray and sad. Put your buns in the toaster.

• Cook the patties without touching them until the bottoms get a crusty char. Flip 'em. If you want your burger medium-rare, now's the time to put the cheese on the charred side. Wait a few minutes to add the cheese for a medium burger and a few minutes longer than that for medium-well. If you want your burger medium-well, add a splash of water to the pan so the patties cook through.

• Once the middle's done to your liking, use a spatula to flip the burger, cheese side down, onto your bottom bun. Yup, that's right. Put the cheese on the bottom. That's Matthew's contribution to my technique. He realized that his condiments always slid around on his melty cheese. This way, the burger won't move and the toppings won't either, and you get the added bonus of having a burger that's also sort of like a grilled cheese. Don't worry—all those meaty juices are still gonna run into the bottom bun.

• If you're not on a diet, put your top bun, split side down, in the fat in the pan. While that's soakin' up beefy goodness, spread mayo and mustard on the meat and stack the lettuce, onion, tomato, and pickles on top. Smoosh the hot top bun over the stack and take a huge bite. Yum.

Mini Meaty Pitas with Cucumber Yogurt Sauce

Serves 4

One summer, I cooked for an Iranian family in Falmouth, Massachusetts (the closest I've ever come to summering on Cape Cod!). I worked crazy hard, but I loved the family. They were from England, but they had held on to their Persian heritage, largely through their food. At first, I was intimidated by their huge collection of Persian cookbooks, but I figured cooking for them was the best place to experiment with this cuisine. If I messed up, I could get help from people who really knew the food and the techniques. Because it was a hot summer, they requested lighter dishes. I created these pitas as an alternative to typical barbecue dishes that weigh you down. I love this with beef, but it works well with turkey or lamb, too. (Just season more aggressively with cumin and chile if you're using lamb.) This dish is a tribute to that family and our summer together. I can't thank them enough for introducing me to a world of flavors that I enjoy to this day.

Cucumber Yogurt Sauce

½ seedless cucumber, peeled and finely diced

½ cup plain whole-milk yogurt

½ cup sour cream

1 garlic clove, minced

1 teaspoon ground cumin

1 teaspoon freshly grated lime zest

Kosher salt and freshly ground black pepper

Burgers

1¼ pounds coarsely ground beef chuck (80% lean)

2 garlic cloves, minced

2 teaspoons fresh mint leaves, chopped, or ½ teaspoon dried mint

2 teaspoons fresh cilantro leaves, chopped, or ½ teaspoon dried cilantro

½ teaspoon ground cinnamon

½ teaspoon freshly grated lime zest

1 teaspoon fresh lime juice

2 tablespoons canola oil, plus more for cooking

1 teaspoon kosher salt

1½ teaspoons freshly ground black pepper

4 pocketless pitas

2 tablespoons dried thyme

1 tablespoon ground sumac (optional)

2 teaspoons sesame seeds, toasted

½ teaspoon table salt

Extra virgin olive oil

2 tomatoes, cored, seeded, and diced

½ seedless cucumber, peeled, seeded, and finely diced

1 To make the sauce: In a bowl, stir together the cucumber, yogurt, sour cream, garlic, cumin, and lime zest. Season to taste with salt and pepper. Let stand for at least 1 hour before serving, or refrigerate in an airtight container for up to 1 day. Stir well before serving.

2 To make the burgers: In a large bowl, gently mix the beef, garlic, mint, cilantro, cinnamon, lime zest and juice, oil, salt, and pepper until well combined. Form the mixture into eight 2-inch-diameter patties.

3 Heat a thin layer of oil in a large cast-iron skillet over medium-high heat. Add a few patties. They should fit comfortably in a single layer; don't crowd the pan. If necessary, cook in batches. Cook until browned on the bottom, about 4 minutes. Then flip them and cook until the meat is cooked through, about 4 minutes longer.

4 Meanwhile, use a 2-inch round cookie cutter to cut 8 rounds out of the pitas. (Snack on the trimmings!) In a small bowl, combine the thyme, sumac, sesame seeds, and salt. Brush the pita rounds with olive oil, then press the spice mixture onto them. Grill or toast the pitas until just warm.

5 Put a patty on each pita, then dollop a spoonful of the sauce on top. Garnish with the tomatoes and cucumber, and serve immediately.

Carla's Tips

• For classic American burgers, I prefer my meat medium-rare. But with these rich spices, I like the flavor of the meat cooked all the way through.

Merguez Lamb Burgers with Feta

Serves 4

Super spicy and juicy, these decadent patties have that ka-pow! effect. If you love lamb and you love bold, gutsy spices and chiles, then this is the burger for you. Regular buns can't handle these hearty patties—you need rolls that have a little crust to support them, but not ones that are too hard or crusty.

1 tablespoon extra virgin olive oil

1/2 cup finely diced yellow onion

2 garlic cloves, minced

1/2 cup jarred green chiles, finely diced

1/2 teaspoon ground cumin

1/2 teaspoon ground coriander

1/2 teaspoon ground cinnamon

1/2 teaspoon kosher salt

1/2 teaspoon freshly ground black pepper

12 ounces coarsely ground lamb

12 ounces Merguez sausage, removed
   from casings and crumbled

1 tablespoon green chile hot sauce

1/2 cup Dijonnaise (see Carla's Tips)

2 teaspoons finely chopped fresh mint
   leaves

4 ciabatta or torta rolls, split and toasted

1/2 cup crumbled feta cheese

1 cucumber, sliced

1 Heat the oil in a small skillet over medium heat. Add the onion and cook, stirring occasionally, until lightly browned, about 3 minutes. Add the garlic, chiles, cumin, coriander, cinnamon, salt, and pepper. Cook, stirring, for 1 minute. Transfer to a bowl and let cool slightly.

2 Add the lamb, sausage, and hot sauce to the bowl and mix gently until well combined. You may need to squish the sausage between your fingertips to break it down into pieces the same size as the ground lamb. Form the mixture into 4 patties the same shape as your bread, making them a little larger than the bread.

3 Heat a large cast-iron skillet over medium-high heat. Add a few patties. They should fit comfortably in a single layer; don't crowd the pan. Cook until browned on the bottom, about 5 minutes, then flip and cook until the meat is cooked through, about 5 minutes longer. Repeat with the remaining patties, draining fat from the pan between batches.

4 While the patties cook, mix the Dijonnaise and mint in a small bowl. Spread this on the cut sides of the rolls.

5 Transfer the patties to the bottom halves of the rolls, top with the feta, cucumber, and the tops of the rolls, and serve immediately.

• •

Carla's Tips

• Dijonnaise is equal parts Dijon mustard and mayo. You can buy it that way or make your own.

• •

Turning Point

Culinary school changed my life in so many ways. I went there out of my love for food, but also because I wanted to really create something, to make something with my hands. The spreadsheets I had run as an accountant didn't quite do it for me. Neither had struttin' down the runways as a model in Milan.

On our designated sausage lesson day, we were told to pull all the ingredients we'd need to make Merguez sausage. I had never heard of it and was shocked to see that we needed to line up thirteen ingredients. But when we made the mix, I was surprised at how straightforward it was. There were a lot of spices, but they were so well balanced, no one flavor dominated another.

That was the easy part. When our teacher pulled out the natural sausage casing, my eyes widened. It had never occurred to me to think about what sausages are stuffed into. (Spoiler alert: lamb intestines!) Natural casings taste great when cooked; they have a nice snap to them. But stuffing a meat mix into them is tricky. They're very delicate, so you have to avoid tearing them. I got into a groove and enjoyed the feel of filling and tying the Merguez.

At the end of that day, I thought, "Wow! This is awesome. I really know something! I've just acquired an actual skill." That was a turning point for me. Those spicy sausages helped me realize that I wanted to take my love of food further. I wanted to keep learning other dishes from all over the world and to push the limits of what I could do in the kitchen. And I'm still doin' it now.

Banh Mi Pork Burgers with Cucumber, Carrots, and Cilantro

Serves 4

Being a Top Chef *contestant can be grueling and exhausting and crazy fun. When we're all wiped out from nonstop competition, we do what we do best: eat good food. Some of my most memorable meals with those talented chefs involved banh mi, traditional Vietnamese sandwiches that layer cured meats, sausages, and pickled vegetables in small, soft versions of French baguettes. I love anything with pickles and fresh cilantro! I've put those flavors in a burger patty here and sand-wiched them in my favorite French roll: buttery brioche. The rich bread makes all the difference, as does high-quality pork.*

¹/₂ **cup julienned peeled carrots**

¹/₂ **cup julienned peeled daikon radish**

2 teaspoons fresh lime juice

1 teaspoon sugar

Kosher salt

1 pound ground pork

¹/₄ **cup very thinly sliced scallions (green onions)**

1 tablespoon freshly grated lime zest

1 garlic clove, minced

1 teaspoon grated peeled fresh ginger

Canola oil, for the pan

Mayonnaise

4 brioche buns, split and toasted

12 fresh cilantro sprigs

1. In a medium bowl, toss the carrots, daikon, lime juice, sugar, and ½ teaspoon salt. Let stand while you make the burgers.

2. In a large bowl, combine the pork, scallions, lime zest, garlic, ginger, and ½ teaspoon salt with your hands until well mixed. Form into four ½-inch-thick patties that are slightly larger than your buns.

3. Heat a large cast-iron skillet over medium heat. Rub it with oil to coat. Add a few patties. They should fit comfortably in a single layer; don't crowd the pan. Cook until browned on the bottom, about 5 minutes, then flip and cook until the meat is cooked through, about 5 minutes longer. Repeat with the remaining patties.

4. Spread mayonnaise on both sides of the buns. Place a patty on each bottom bun, and top with the cilantro, carrots, and daikon. Sandwich with the top buns and serve immediately.

. . . .

Carla's Tips

• To grate ginger without getting its stringy fibers, grate it lengthwise, along the fibers.

• **Swap Out:** You can use ground dark meat chicken instead of pork.

• **Some Like It Hot:** Squirt sriracha all over the burgers. And if you really like cilantro, mince a bunch and mix it with the mayo.

. . . .

Baked Casseroles

Comfort food at its best comes in a casserole. It's just so homey, with the meat, veggies, and starches all smooshed together and baked until bubbly. There are a lot of components to casseroles, but the beauty of them is that they can be left alone in the oven once they're assembled.

 ITALIAN-AMERICAN

Tomato Meat Sauce

Makes about 8 cups

An oldie but goodie here. There are a million and one things you can do to a basic meat and tomato sauce, but I like to keep it simple and keep it classic. That way, I can use it in just about any dish, from a simple plate of spaghetti to Meat Lasagna (page 141) to baked penne to roasted eggplant.

1 tablespoon extra virgin olive oil

2 medium yellow onions, very finely diced

Kosher salt

4 garlic cloves, minced

1 pound ground beef chuck (80% lean)

1 teaspoon dried oregano

2 tablespoons tomato paste

Two 28-ounce cans diced or crushed fire-roasted tomatoes

1 Heat the oil in a large Dutch oven over medium heat. Add the onions and ½ teaspoon salt and cook, stirring occasionally, for 2 minutes. Then add the garlic and cook, stirring, until the onions are translucent, about 4 minutes.

2 Push the onions to one side of pan and add the beef to the other. Raise the heat to high, sprinkle beef with 1 teaspoon salt, and cook, stirring to break up the meat into small chunks, until browned, about 5 minutes. Drain in a fine-mesh sieve.

3 Return the meat mixture to the Dutch oven over high heat. Add the oregano and tomato paste. Cook, stirring, for 1 minute, then stir in the tomatoes with their juices. Boil for 5 minutes, and then season with salt to taste. The sauce needs to be thin for lasagna so that the noodles can soak up the juices. If you prefer a thicker sauce for other pasta dishes or polenta, just keep simmering.

• •

Carla's Tips

• Used diced tomatoes if you prefer a sauce with chunks or crushed tomatoes for a smoother sauce. You can also do a blend for a texture somewhere in between.

• •

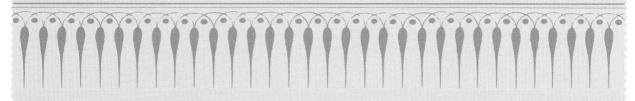

A Labor of Love

My first boyfriend, Tony, was a classmate at Howard. I think it's safe to say I liked his family as much as I did him. (Even today, I still chat with his mom occasionally.) When I visited his folks deep in the Virginia countryside, I was always so relaxed. His parents spoiled me; they knew how much I love peas and carrots, so they'd keep a stash just for me.

One Saturday, while they were all out running errands, I decided to cook for them. Mind you, I didn't know how to cook, but I knew Tony liked lasagna. So I figured I'd make it for him and his family.

I found a recipe in one of his mom's cookbooks, made a shopping list, and headed for the store. I didn't have a car, so I started walking. Even though they lived in the country, I didn't fully appreciate how far away everything was. I made it there fine, but getting home was another thing. The grocery bags were heavy and the cows mooing at me along the way somehow made the trip harder. When I was within sight of their house, one of their neighbors pulled up next to me and shouted, "Hey Carla! You want a ride?" I gritted my teeth and answered sweetly, "Oh no, I'm fine. Thank you though!"

At that point, I was determined to do it myself. No way did I need a ride! I'd walked that far, I was going to go all the way. And I did and I made a fantastic lasagna too.

At the end of the meal, his mom asked how I'd gotten all of the ingredients. When I told her I had walked, her jaw dropped. "Carla! It's five miles to the store and five miles back!" I hadn't realized it was that far. Can you talk about putting love in your cooking? All I kept thinking about was how I wanted to make something special for someone. Sometimes, cooking a meal is a lot of work and a lot of hassle. When I say it's worth it, I'm not just talkin' about how good everything tastes at the end. I'm talkin' about making a meal a labor of love. I can't think of a better way to show someone how much you care.

IRISH

Shepherd's Pie
Serves 8

When I was running my Lunch Bunch catering business, I cooked weekly specials inspired by meals from my London days. The first time I attempted shepherd's pie, I didn't know you couldn't make mashed potatoes in a food processor and made a complete mess. Oh, the glueyness of those spuds! For super creamy potatoes, you have to use a ricer or a food mill. (You can also use a potato masher, but they'll be chunkier.) Sure, this is a meat dish, but the creamy, crusty browned potatoes on top are the star to me.

8 medium Yukon gold potatoes, peeled

Kosher salt

1 tablespoon extra virgin olive oil

2 medium yellow onions, diced

4 garlic cloves, minced

2 pounds ground lamb

1 cup diced carrots

1 teaspoon minced fresh rosemary leaves

Freshly ground black pepper

¼ cup all-purpose flour

2 cups Chicken Stock (page 103) or store-bought unsalted chicken broth

2 teaspoons Worcestershire sauce

1 cup fresh or thawed frozen peas

½ cup heavy cream, heated

8 tablespoons (1 stick) unsalted butter, at room temperature

1. Place the potatoes in a large pot and add enough cold water to cover by 2 inches. Generously salt the water and bring to a boil over high heat. Reduce the heat and simmer until the potatoes are very soft, about 40 minutes.

2. Meanwhile, heat the oil in a large, deep cast-iron skillet over medium-high heat. Add the onions and ½ teaspoon salt and cook, stirring occasionally, for 2 minutes. Then add the garlic and cook, stirring, until the onions are translucent, about 4 minutes.

3. Push the onions to one side of the pan and add the lamb to the other. Raise the heat to high, sprinkle the lamb with 1 teaspoon salt, and cook, stirring to break up the meat into small chunks, until browned, about 10 minutes. Stir in the carrots, rosemary, and 1 teaspoon pepper. Cook, stirring occasionally, until the carrots are crisp-tender, about 5 minutes. Drain in a fine-mesh sieve, and return to the pan.

4 Add the flour and cook, stirring, for 1 minute. Stir in the chicken stock and Worcestershire sauce and bring to a simmer. If using fresh peas, add them now. Simmer, stirring occasionally, for 15 minutes.

5 While the meat's simmering, drain the potatoes. Put them through a ricer or food mill into a large bowl, and add the cream, butter, and ½ teaspoon salt. Fold until smooth and silky.

6 Set the broiler rack 6 inches from the heat source. Preheat the broiler.

7 Stir the frozen peas, if using, into the simmering meat. Dollop the mashed potatoes over the meat to cover the top. Transfer the skillet to the broiler and broil just until the potatoes are golden brown, about 3 minutes. Serve hot.

· ·

Carla's Tips

• Yes, there's a lot of butter and cream in my mashed potatoes, but I always like that rich goodness in there. You could use less or stir in stock instead if you prefer a lighter topping.

· ·

MEXICAN

Beef and Pepper Enchiladas

Serves 8

Even though I ate a lot of enchiladas growing up, I didn't have authentic ones until I made them for a catering job for Choice Hotels. My colleague Lynn Foster showed me the secret to true enchiladas: You dunk the tortillas in hot oil before filling them, rolling them, and slathering them with sauce. That prevents the tortillas from getting soggy and absorbing all the sauce. I have to confess that I skipped that step here to make these enchiladas easier, but also because I sort of like it when the tortillas soften and meld into the filling and sauce. If you prefer firmer tortillas, immerse the tortillas, one at a time, into hot oil in a skillet until softened but not crisp, about 5 seconds. Then fill, roll, and bake as directed below.

Chile Sauce

4 dried red Mexican chiles, rinsed

2 tablespoons canola oil

1 medium yellow onion, diced

Kosher salt

2 garlic cloves, sliced

1 cup diced fire-roasted tomatoes

1 teaspoon cider vinegar

1 teaspoon dried oregano

1 cup hot water

Enchiladas

2 medium red bell peppers

2 large poblano chiles

1 tablespoon extra virgin olive oil

2 medium yellow onions, very thinly sliced

Kosher salt

4 garlic cloves, very thinly sliced

1 pound ground beef chuck (80% lean)

2 teaspoons ground cumin

1 teaspoon dried oregano

Freshly ground black pepper

16 corn tortillas, warmed until pliable

1 1/2 cups crumbled queso fresco

1 To make the chile sauce: In a medium saucepan, heat the chiles over medium heat, turning, until toasted and fragrant, about 2 minutes. Remove from the pan and discard the stems and the seeds.

2 Add the oil, onion, and 1/2 teaspoon salt to the saucepan. Cook, stirring occasionally, until the onion is just translucent, about 2 minutes. Add the garlic and cook, stirring, until tender, about 2 minutes.

3 Add the tomatoes and chiles and boil, stirring, until the liquid evaporates, about 2 minutes. Stir in the vinegar, oregano, and water. Bring to a boil, then reduce the heat and simmer for 5 minutes. Transfer to a blender and puree until very smooth. Strain through a fine-mesh sieve and season to taste with salt. Use immediately or refrigerate in an airtight container for up to 3 days.

(continued on next page)

4 To make the enchiladas: Preheat the oven to 350°F.

5 If you happen to have an outdoor grill heated to high, grill the bell peppers and poblanos until evenly charred. Otherwise, turn your stove's gas burners on medium-high and set the peppers directly on the grate. Cook, turning occasionally, until they are blackened and blistered all over. Transfer to a bowl, cover with plastic wrap, and let sit until cool enough to handle. Discard the stems, seeds, skin, and inner ribs. Thinly slice the peppers and chiles.

6 Heat the oil in a Dutch oven or flameproof casserole over medium heat. Add the onions and ½ teaspoon salt. Cook, stirring occasionally, until the onions are just translucent, about 2 minutes. Add the garlic, raise the heat to high, and then add the beef and ½ teaspoon salt. Cook, stirring and breaking up the beef into small bits, until browned, about 5 minutes.

7 Add the cumin, oregano, peppers, and chiles. Cook, stirring, for 1 minute. Season to taste with salt and pepper, and remove from the heat.

8 Spread a thin layer of sauce in the bottom of a shallow 3-quart casserole or baking dish. Put 2 heaping tablespoons of the beef mixture in a tortilla and roll it up. Place the roll in the pan, seam side down. Repeat with the remaining tortillas and beef. Pour the remaining sauce all over the enchiladas, and top with the cheese. Bake until the sauce bubbles and the cheese melts, about 20 minutes. Serve hot.

Serve with Tangy Hot Cabbage Slaw (page 14).

Carla's Tips

• To warm and soften the tortillas, spread them out on a baking sheet and bake at 350°F, turning them once, until pliable, about 3 minutes.

• Watch the toasting chiles carefully! They go from golden brown to burned in the blink of an eye.

• This is good for making ahead for guests. You can assemble the whole thing, then bake it when you're ready to serve it.

• **Some Like It Hot**: Keep the seeds in the poblano chile.

• **Swap Out:** Use pulled cooked chicken instead of the beef. Stir it in with the peppers until just heated through.

• You can use mild feta cheese or freshly grated Monterey Jack in place of the queso fresco.

 ITALIAN-AMERICAN

Meat Lasagna

Serves 12

You just gotta do it. Yes, a lasagna takes time and usually makes a bit of a mess, but it's just a big ol' tray of comfort. I'm sticking to the American adaptation, using ricotta in place of a cream sauce, but I insist on fresh mozzarella. It's creamier and more flavorful than the drier, spongy balls. I love cheese, but I find that full layers of both ricotta and mozz are over the top. I alternate dollops of ricotta with mozzarella slices, then swap their positions the next time I'm at the cheese layer. That way, you get both cheeses in each bite, but not a gut-busting double dose.

12 no-boil lasagna noodles

One 15-ounce container ricotta cheese

1 cup finely grated Parmigiano-Reggiano cheese, plus more for topping

2 large eggs, beaten

¼ cup very thinly sliced fresh parsley leaves

¼ teaspoon freshly grated nutmeg

Kosher salt and freshly ground black pepper

Tomato Meat Sauce (page 134), warmed

1 pound fresh mozzarella, cut in half and thinly sliced

¼ cup very thinly sliced fresh basil leaves

1 Preheat the oven to 350°F. In a large dish, soak the noodles in cold water for a few minutes, then drain.

2 In a large bowl, stir together the ricotta, Parmigiano-Reggiano, eggs, parsley, nutmeg, and ½ teaspoon each salt and pepper.

3 Now for the fun part: Build your lasagna! In a 3-quart (9 by 13 by 3-inch) baking dish, spread 1 heaping cup of the tomato sauce. Arrange 4 noodles on top, spacing them ½ inch apart, and spoon 2 cups of sauce on top. Dollop spoonfuls of half of the ricotta mixture on top, spacing the mounds 2 inches apart, and then put a third of the mozzarella slices in the spaces between the ricotta dollops. Top with 4 noodles, 2 cups sauce, the remaining ricotta, and another third of the mozzarella, alternating the position of the cheeses this time so that the ricotta dollops are on top of the first layer of mozzarella slices and vice versa. Spoon 2 cups sauce over the cheese, top with 4 noodles, and spoon the remaining sauce on top. Arrange the remaining mozzarella over the sauce.

4 Cover the baking dish with parchment paper, then foil, and bake for 30 minutes. Uncover and continue baking until bubbling and very hot throughout, about 15 minutes.

5 Top the lasagna with the basil and sprinkle with Parmigiano-Reggiano. Let stand for at least 10 minutes before slicing.

Roasts

You want to impress? Do a roast. That big ol' hunk of meat looks awesome on a buffet and is super easy to cook to perfection. One big secret is to make sure the roast isn't stone cold as it's going into the oven. That'll cause the meat to cook unevenly. The other is to buy a meat thermometer. Seasoned chefs can tell if a roast is cooked to their desired doneness by pressing the meat with their fingertips. If you're not quite there yet, insert a meat thermometer into the thickest part of the roast to see if you've nailed your ideal temp.

 GREEK

Roasted Leg of Lamb with Fennel

Serves 10

When I was a private chef in the Bahamas, I cooked lamb all the time. The family I worked for was British and they loved nothing more than a good roast lamb. (Well, since it was the Bahamas, I often grilled it on the beach to serve at their outdoor parties.) Instead of using milder British seasonings, I always went Greek with lamb and made sure there was plenty of garlic to complement the rich meat. As much as I love grilled lamb, I enjoy roasting it even more because I can stick sweet veggies in the pan and let them soak up all the meaty juices while they caramelize. It makes an awesome one-pan meal.

2 tablespoons extra virgin olive oil

1 tablespoon finely chopped fresh oregano leaves

1 tablespoon finely chopped fresh mint leaves

1 teaspoon ground cinnamon

2 teaspoons ground fennel seeds

10 garlic cloves: 4 minced, 6 smashed

Kosher salt and freshly ground black pepper

One 4½-pound butterflied boneless leg of lamb

2 medium yellow onions, cut into thin wedges

1 fennel bulb, stalk chopped, bulb cut into thin wedges

2 fresh or dried bay leaves

¼ cup Chicken Stock (page 103) or store-bought unsalted chicken broth

1 In a small bowl, combine the oil, oregano, mint, cinnamon, fennel seeds, minced garlic, 2 teaspoons salt, and ½ teaspoon pepper. Rub this all over the lamb, cover with plastic wrap, and refrigerate for at least 2 hours and up to overnight. Let the lamb stand at room temperature for 1 hour before cooking.

2 Preheat the oven to 450°F. Scatter the onion, fennel bulb and stalk, bay leaves, and smashed garlic in a large roasting pan and season with a pinch each of salt and pepper. Place a roasting rack over the vegetables and add the stock to the pan. Place the lamb on the rack.

3 Roast for 20 minutes. Then reduce the heat to 350°F and continue roasting until the lamb registers 150°F for medium, about 25 minutes. Discard the bay leaves. Let the lamb rest for 15 minutes, then slice it and serve with the pan vegetables and juices.

Serve with Cucumber Yogurt Sauce (page 128) and warm pitas.

Carla's Tips

• Normally, I cook my meat to medium-rare, sometimes going even rarer than that. But for leg of lamb, I prefer the meat medium. Otherwise, I find it too chewy and, well, fleshy. You can decrease or increase the cooking time to your taste. Just be sure to keep checking the temperature with a meat thermometer to avoid overcooking.

Spice-Rubbed Beef Roast with Potatoes and Carrots

Serves 10

I haven't yet had a chance to travel to Morocco, but ever since I had a phenomenal meal at a newly opened Moroccan restaurant in D.C., I've been fascinated by North African flavors. Here I've borrowed those spices for a quintessentially American roast beef. Flavoring a really familiar cut of meat with different seasonings is just plain fun.

2 tablespoons minced fresh mint leaves

2 tablespoons extra virgin olive oil

1 tablespoon ground cumin

1 tablespoon ground coriander

1/2 teaspoon ground cardamom

1/2 teaspoon cayenne pepper

2 teaspoons kosher salt

1 teaspoon freshly ground black pepper

One 5-pound top round beef roast

1 large yellow onion, cut into 1/2-inch-thick rings

4 large carrots, peeled and cut into 1-inch chunks

8 small Yukon gold potatoes, scrubbed and cut into 1-inch chunks

2 cups unsalted beef stock, plus more if needed

1/2 cup sliced pitted green olives or oil-cured black olives

1/4 cup store-bought preserved lemon, chopped

1 In a small bowl, combine the mint, oil, cumin, coriander, cardamom, cayenne, salt, and pepper. Rub this all over the beef, cover with plastic wrap, and refrigerate for at least 4 hours and up to overnight. Let the beef stand at room temperature for 1 hour before cooking.

2 Preheat the oven to 400°F. Fit a roasting rack into a large roasting pan. Scatter the onion, carrots, and potatoes around or under the rack, then place the beef on the rack. Add enough stock to reach 1/2 inch up the sides of the pan.

3 Roast for 20 minutes. Reduce heat to 350°F and continue roasting until the beef registers 130°F for medium-rare, about 1 hour and 10 minutes.

4 Transfer the beef and vegetables to a serving platter. Stir the olives and preserved lemon into the pan juices, and serve the sauce with the beef and vegetables.

. . . .

Carla's Tips

• If you prefer a thicker sauce, straddle the roasting pan over two burners after you've transferred the beef and vegetables to a platter. Bring the liquid to a boil and boil until slightly thickened. Then stir in the olives and lemon.

• **Swap Out:** If you don't have preserved lemon, use the grated zest and juice of 1 lemon instead.

. . . .

 HUNGARIAN

Poppy-Seed Pork Tenderloin with Fresh Herb Crust

Serves 4

Chef Curtis Stone came on The Chew *as a guest and did this quirky thing to his roast: He finished cooking it, then he coated it with minced fresh herbs. I had used that technique on goat cheese before, but never thought to try it with meat. That hit of freshness over the rich meat was amazing. I said to him, "Oh, child, that's worth stealing." I wasn't kidding! Here, I've decided to add another layer of flavor by spice-rubbing the meat before cooking it and then coating it with the herb mix after. It tastes so complex, but it's so easy! Thank you, Curtis.*

1 tablespoon canola oil

1 teaspoon sweet paprika

1 teaspoon poppy seeds

1/2 teaspoon ground cinnamon

1/2 teaspoon kosher salt

1/4 teaspoon freshly ground white pepper

1 whole (12- to 14-ounce) pork tenderloin

1/4 cup finely chopped fresh dill leaves

1/4 cup finely chopped fresh flat-leaf parsley leaves

1 Preheat the oven to 425°F. Meanwhile, combine the oil, paprika, poppy seeds, cinnamon, salt, and white pepper in a small bowl. Rub this all over the pork and let stand on a rimmed baking sheet at room temperature until the oven is ready.

2 Roast the pork until it registers 135°F for medium, about 15 minutes.

3 While the pork is roasting, tear a sheet of parchment paper the length of the tenderloin. Sprinkle the dill and parsley in an even layer on the paper.

4 Roll the cooked pork in its pan juices, then transfer it to the fresh herbs and roll it in the herbs to coat evenly. Let the pork stand for 5 minutes, then cut into slices at an angle and serve.

• •

Carla's Tips

• If your tenderloin has a tapered end that's half the thickness of the rest of the loin, tuck it under for even cooking. Or you can leave it and serve it to anyone who prefers their pork really well done.

• •

Short Ribs

This magic cut of meat packs so much flavor. I love that you can cook down big pieces until they're fork-tender or quick-grill thin slices for ribs with a pleasant chew. The richness takes to just about any seasoning, but simple is better here. Short ribs have been all the rage in restaurants in recent years, but I think they're worth doing at home. The hardest part is buying the right cut. For the braises here, you want 3-inch squares with the bone in. That means that if a butcher has a whole rack of short ribs, he needs to cut between the bones, then cut across the bones to form 3-inch square pieces. For the grilled dish, the butcher will have to cut across the whole rack, through all 3 or 4 of the bones, making ½-inch-wide slices.

KOREAN

Grilled Soy-Marinated Short Ribs

Serves 10

The summer after my college graduation, I traveled to Seoul with my friend Lorrie and tasted Korean barbecue for the first time. I thought it was so cool to get to barbecue my meat myself, right on the tabletop. It was very festive, even though it was just the two of us at the table with tons of dishes. In lieu of a tabletop setup at home, I grill my ribs on my charcoal grill for a great smoky flavor, and on an indoor grill pan when I'm craving this in bad weather.

The salty, sweet marinade has a garlicky kick that comes through the char of the meat. The hardest part about this dish is buying the right ribs. Unlike short ribs cut for braising, these are cut into ¹/₂-inch-thick slices through three or four bones and are labeled "flanken-style" in Western markets and "L.A.-style" in Korean ones. At my local market, I asked my butcher to cut his whole slab of short ribs into the slices for me and he kindly did. I bet your butcher will do the same.

³/₄ **cup soy sauce**

³/₄ **cup water**

³/₄ **cup minced yellow onion**

¹/₄ **cup minced garlic**

¹/₄ **cup packed light or dark brown sugar**

3 **tablespoons cider vinegar**

2 **teaspoons toasted sesame oil**

1 **teaspoon freshly ground black pepper**

Twenty ¹/₂-inch-thick flanken-style short ribs (4¹/₃ pounds total)

1 In a medium bowl, stir together the soy sauce, water, onion, garlic, brown sugar, vinegar, sesame oil, and pepper. Divide the ribs between two gallon-size heavy-duty resealable plastic bags, and then divide the marinade between the bags. Make sure the marinade is evenly distributed among the ribs. Seal tightly and refrigerate for at least 6 hours and up to overnight.

2 Prepare an outdoor grill for high-heat grilling (charcoal will make the tastiest ribs!), or heat a cast-iron skillet over medium-high heat. For both, cook the ribs, turning once, until nicely browned on both sides, about 5 minutes total.

Serve with short-grain white rice and kimchi.

Red Wine and Tomato Braised Short Ribs

Serves 6

For this stovetop braise, the ribs get an herb salt rub and a sear to seal in those flavors. You don't do much after that—just let it simmer away. I've been making Italian short ribs for years, but I always learn something new from my Chew *co-host Mario Batali. In this case, it was his unique way of plating: He spreads warm polenta all over a wooden board, then nestles the ribs in it and sprinkles the gremolata on top. That rustic look reflects just how warming this meal tastes.*

Gremolata

¹/₄ cup finely chopped fresh flat-leaf parsley leaves

1 teaspoon minced fresh thyme leaves

¹/₂ teaspoon minced fresh rosemary leaves

2 tablespoons freshly grated lemon zest

2 garlic cloves, minced

¹/₄ teaspoon kosher salt

Short Ribs

2 teaspoons minced fresh rosemary leaves

2 teaspoons chopped fresh thyme leaves

Kosher salt and freshly ground black pepper

Eight 3-inch pieces bone-in short ribs (2³/₄ pounds total)

1 large yellow onion, finely chopped

4 garlic cloves, peeled

2 tablespoons tomato paste

¹/₂ cup dry red wine

2 cups unsalted beef stock

1 To make the gremolata: In a bowl, rub the ingredients with your fingertips to mix.

2 To make the short ribs: Rub the rosemary, thyme, 1½ teaspoons salt, and ½ teaspoon black pepper all over the ribs. Let sit for 1 hour.

3 Heat a large, wide Dutch oven over medium-high heat. Add the short ribs, fat side down, in a single layer, spacing the ribs apart. Don't crowd the pan; work in batches if you have to. Cook, turning once, until browned, about 4 minutes. Transfer to a plate.

4 Drain the fat from the pan, leaving a thin film behind, and add the onion and garlic. Reduce the heat to low. Cook, stirring and scraping the browned bits from the bottom of the pan, until the onions are lightly browned, about 5 minutes. Add the tomato paste and cook, stirring, for 2 minutes.

5 Add the wine, raise the heat to high, and cook until almost completely evaporated. Add the stock, bring to a boil, and then adjust the heat to maintain a steady simmer. Nestle the ribs in the vegetables in a single layer, bone side down. Partially cover and simmer until fork-tender, about 3 hours. Top with the gremolata and serve.

Serve over Parmigiano-Reggiano Polenta (page 69).

 SOUTHERN

Caramelized Onion Short Ribs

Serves 6

The flavor's in the brown here. It's a super simple dish and so, so satisfying. Back home in Nashville, this was a big Sunday supper thing that Daddy and Grandma Thelma made together. I've kept their basic onion-carrot-garlic formula, but streamlined the recipe by browning the ribs in the oven while I prep the veg. Then the whole thing hangs out in the oven until the meat's falling off the bone. I can't imagine a better easy family meal.

Kosher salt

Eight 3-inch pieces bone-in short ribs (2³/₄ pounds total)

1 tablespoon canola oil

5 medium carrots, peeled and cut into ¹/₂-inch chunks

2 medium yellow onions, cut into thin half-moons

6 garlic cloves, peeled

1 fresh or dried bay leaf

4 cups unsalted beef stock, plus more if needed

1 Preheat the oven to 400°F. Generously salt both sides of the short ribs and place them, meat side up, in a single layer on a rimmed baking sheet. Roast until browned, about 15 minutes.

2 Meanwhile, in a large, wide Dutch oven or flameproof casserole, heat the oil over medium-high heat. Add the carrots, onions, and garlic and spread them out in an even layer. Let sit until browned on the bottom, about 3 minutes, then stir and spread again. Let sit until the bottom is nicely colored again, about 3 minutes. Sprinkle with ½ teaspoon salt and stir well.

3 Add the bay leaf and stock and cook, stirring and scraping the browned bits from the pan, until boiling. Simmer until the short ribs are ready.

4 When the short ribs are browned, nestle the pieces in the vegetables in a single layer. Cover and transfer to the oven.

5 Reduce the oven temperature to 350°F. Bake for 1 hour.

6 Turn the ribs over, add more stock if the mixture is drying out, and bake until the ribs are fork-tender, about 2 hours longer. Skim off and discard the excess fat from the sauce. Discard the bay leaf and serve hot.

Serve over Creamy Cheese Grits (page 68).

Rice and Beans

What normally serves as a side dish is even better as a main when just a little meat is thrown in. The meat's not the star here, but it adds a lot to the subtlety of starchy rice and beans. You can drop the meat from any of these recipes to make them vegetarian, but know that the dishes will lose some depth and complexity. When I can, I like to cook beans from their dried state, but sometimes I just don't have time for that. If you do, by all means do it! Soak the dried beans for about 6 hours, then simmer with the aromatics until just tender.

 SOUTHERN

Red Beans and Rice

Serves 4

New Orleans cuisine is all about the holy trinity of onion, celery, and green bell pepper. You start this dish, as with so many others, with equal parts of each, and then you build on that foundation. Traditionally this is made with pickled pork, which is hard to find anywhere outside of Louisiana. To replicate the unique depth of flavor that ingredient brings, I combine cider vinegar with a ham hock. Together, they contribute a meaty tang to the mix.

2 tablespoons canola oil

1 cup finely diced yellow onion

1 cup finely diced celery

1 cup finely diced green bell pepper

Kosher salt

2 garlic cloves, minced

1 ham hock, skin discarded, meat cut into ¹/₂-inch chunks, bone reserved

1 fresh or dried bay leaf

¹/₂ teaspoon dried thyme

¹/₂ teaspoon crushed red chile flakes

Freshly ground black pepper

4 cups Chicken Stock (page 103) or store-bought unsalted chicken broth

1 tablespoon cider vinegar

Two 15-ounce cans red beans, preferably small, rinsed and drained

Perfect Baked Rice (page 71), preferably made with Carolina white rice

(continued on next page)

1 Heat the oil in a large saucepan over medium-high heat. Add the onion, celery, bell pepper, and 1 teaspoon salt and cook, stirring occasionally, until fragrant, about 1 minute. Add the garlic and cook, stirring, for 1 minute. Add the ham hock meat and bone, bay leaf, thyme, chile flakes, and ½ teaspoon pepper and cook, stirring, for 2 minutes.

2 Add the broth and vinegar and bring to a boil. Cover, reduce the heat, and simmer for 10 minutes. Stir in the beans and simmer uncovered for 30 minutes. You want the beans really mushy and soft.

3 Discard the ham hock bone and the bay leaf. Transfer ¼ cup of the beans to a small bowl and mash them. Stir back into the pan, and simmer until thickened. Serve over the rice.

. . . .

Carla's Tips

• **Some Like It Hot:** I definitely douse mine with hot sauce. You should, too, if you like heat.

. . . .

The Other South

Red beans and rice is a New Orleans sort of thing that I didn't grow up eating in Nashville. It wasn't until my sister, Kim, went to Xavier for college that I got a taste of it and fell in love with it. During one of my trips to see her, I was in a postcard-collecting phase and bought a stack that had recipes printed on the back. They seemed fun at the time and I squirreled them away with everything else I'd been collecting.

Years later, I found those postcards just as I was starting my Lunch Bunch business. (I'm a total pack rat.) I had the cards for étouffée, bread pudding, and, of course, red beans and rice. Those postcard recipes became the base recipes for my business, and my clients loved them. Even though I'm not a New Orleans native, I came to know the cuisine well by cooking from those cards and tweaking the tastes over the years.

When I got to compete for *Top Chef* in New Orleans, I almost felt like I was going home to cook. Over the years those Cajun and Creole specialties had become a part of who I am as a cook, and I find so much comfort in them today.

 BRAZILIAN

Feijoada: Two-Bean Turkey Stew

Serves 4

Going to Brazil is on my bucket list. Every time I meet Brazilians, I'm struck by how warm and friendly they are. This dish is about taking their comfort food and adding a Carla-ism: in this case, smoked turkey wings. I can picture someone picking up those wings and gnawing on 'em. It's the kind of dish where it's okay to get in there and get dirty. It's kinda like a bean stew, starting with a drop-and-roll stock: Just get everything in there and you can walk away while it simmers. Pork's most commonly used—and a ham hock would taste yummy here—but I really like the smoked turkey in my version. I bet this would be just as tasty with smoked chicken thighs or a good sausage, too.

1 tablespoon extra virgin olive oil

1 cup finely diced yellow onion

¹/₂ cup thinly sliced scallions (green onions), plus more for garnish

2 garlic cloves, minced

Kosher salt

2 smoked turkey wings

1 fresh or dried bay leaf

¹/₂ teaspoon ground coriander

3 cups water

1 medium red bell pepper, stemmed, seeded, and finely diced

One 15-ounce can black beans, rinsed and drained

One 15-ounce can pink beans, rinsed and drained

Perfect Baked Rice (page 71)

4 strips bacon, cooked and crumbled (optional)

1 Heat the oil in a large saucepan over medium heat. Add the onion, scallions, garlic, and 1 teaspoon salt. Cook, stirring frequently, until the onion is tender and translucent, about 5 minutes. Add the turkey wings, bay leaf, coriander, and water. Bring to a boil, then reduce the heat and simmer for 50 minutes.

2 Add the bell pepper and beans, and continue simmering for 10 minutes.

3 Transfer the turkey wings to a cutting board. When they are cool enough to handle, pull off and chop the meat; discard the bones. Return the meat to the simmering liquid.

4 Divide the rice among individual plates and top with the beans, then the bacon if using. Garnish with scallions and serve hot.

• •

Carla's Tips

• **Some Like It Hot:** Sprinkle crushed red chile flakes or hot sauce all over.

• •

Spiced Chickpeas and Lamb with Basmati Rice

Serves 4

Imagine Hamburger Helper with lamb and Middle Eastern spices—that's the level of comfort and yumminess you get in this stirred-up mix of spiced rice and meaty beans. Even though it may look like a lot of spice, it's exactly the right amount. Both rice and beans are starchy enough that they can take a lot of seasoning, and the rich lamb takes to the spices well. Ground lamb's a great way to use a little meat to make an impression and get great flavor. My mom, who doesn't really like lamb, would like this dish because the lamb has friends, rice and beans and spices, that complement it.

2 tablespoons extra virgin olive oil

1 medium yellow onion, very finely diced

Kosher salt

2 garlic cloves, minced

1 medium yellow bell pepper, stemmed, seeded, and diced

1 cup brown basmati rice

2 teaspoons ground cumin

2 teaspoons ground coriander

1 teaspoon cayenne pepper

2 cups water

1 pound ground lamb

Freshly ground black pepper

One 15-ounce can black beans, rinsed and drained

One 15-ounce can chickpeas, rinsed and drained

Chopped fresh cilantro, mint, and flat-leaf parsley leaves, mixed, for serving

1 Heat the oil in a large Dutch oven or flameproof casserole over medium-high heat. Add the onion and ½ teaspoon salt and cook, stirring occasionally, until just tender, about 3 minutes. Add the garlic and cook, stirring, for 1 minute. Add the bell pepper and cook, stirring occasionally, until the onion is translucent, about 5 minutes.

2 Add the rice, cumin, coriander, and cayenne and cook, stirring, for 1 minute. Add the water and bring to a boil. Then cover, reduce the heat to low, and simmer until the rice is just tender, about 30 minutes.

3 Meanwhile, heat a large cast-iron skillet over medium-high heat until hot. Add the lamb and press it into the pan in a single layer. Sprinkle with 1 teaspoon salt and ½ teaspoon pepper. Just let it sit to get some color, about 10 minutes. When it's really browned on the bottom, stir it around to make sure it's all cooked. Drain in a colander.

4 Stir the lamb, black beans, and chickpeas into the rice. Simmer uncovered until heated through, about 5 minutes. Stir in the herbs, and serve.

Carla's Tips

• **Swap Out:** You can use a red or orange bell pepper in place of the yellow.

• White basmati rice works too, and will cook a few minutes faster.

Vegetarian Entrées

Whether I'm preparing a meal for friends and family at home, or cooking professionally, I plan my menu with the intention of making everyone feel special. Of course I like to introduce new flavors, but ultimately I want to make sure everyone gets dishes that they feel are made just for them. That's why I always made vegetarian entrées for my catering gigs—even if I didn't know whether there'd be vegetarians there—and why I always make beautiful veggie main dishes for my dinner parties.

Maybe I'm especially sensitive to vegetarians because I really enjoy eating meatless meals, too. When I go out for barbecue in the South, I load my plate with the sides. My go-to Indian takeout order is a bunch of veggies to go with my rice and naan. There's something deeply satisfying about filling up on flavorful vegetable dishes because there's such a mix of tastes and textures. And there's something really nice about having a showstopper vegetarian main dish that makes everyone at the table—even the carnivores—want a great big helping.

· ·

Beans

I could eat beans all day long, they're so yummy! I *luuuuv* the creamy texture and rich flavors, especially when they're simmered from scratch. But let's get real, folks. I'll admit it: Sometimes (okay, a lot of the time), I pop open a can of beans for my cooking. I wish I had the time or the foresight to simmer dried beans—and sometimes I do—but when I don't, canned really work fine. In the dishes here, there are strong flavors goin' on, so I actually developed the recipes with canned. If you want to cook beans, do! They're tastier, less expensive, and can freeze well too. Soak picked-over dried beans for 6 hours, drain, then simmer in plenty of water with aromatics until tender. Taste to see if they're done. You need 1¾ cups cooked dried beans for each can of beans called for in a recipe. Talk about a desert island ingredient!

Black Bean Picadillo

Serves 4 (makes 3 cups)

Often made with meat, a picadillo combines sweet raisins and tomato with savory garlic and chiles. I think those bold, well-balanced flavors taste just as good without meat. The key is to find a really great chile powder that's ground from whole chiles. Check the labels to watch out for added seasonings—you want the pure thing. I use this to stuff my Black Bean Empanadas (page 166), but it's also great over rice or in tortillas.

½ cup golden raisins

⅔ cup hot water

1 tablespoon canola oil

1½ cups diced yellow onion

2 garlic cloves, thinly sliced

Kosher salt and freshly ground black pepper

1 teaspoon ground Mexican chiles, such as ancho

2 tablespoons tomato paste

One 15-ounce can black beans, rinsed and drained

½ cup fresh or thawed frozen corn kernels

½ cup shredded sharp cheddar, Monterey Jack, or a blend

2 tablespoons chopped fresh cilantro leaves (optional)

1 In a small bowl, cover the raisins with the hot water. Let soak.

2 Heat the oil in a large skillet over medium heat. Add the onion, garlic, ½ teaspoon salt, and ¼ teaspoon pepper. Cook, stirring occasionally, until the onion just starts to turn translucent, about 3 minutes. Add the ground chiles and cook, stirring, for 1 minute. Add the tomato paste and cook, stirring, for 2 minutes.

3 Stir in the beans, corn, and raisins with their soaking liquid. Bring to a boil, then reduce the heat and simmer for 5 minutes.

4 If serving alone or with tortillas or rice, top with the cheese and the cilantro if using. If using as empanada filling, cool completely, then stir in the cheese and the cilantro if using.

Black Bean and Brown Rice Burgers

Serves 4

Flavors from India meet American vegetarian in this hearty burger. Because there's already rice in the burger, I prefer to use thin buns or to dig out the guts of thick buns. Any brown rice will work here, but I really like basmati. If you're not making the rice fresh—and this dish is a great use of leftover rice— just microwave it before mixing the burgers. The heat helps bind the patties together.

5 whole-grain hamburger buns, centers hollowed out a bit if thick

Mayonnaise, for the buns (see Carla's Tips)

One 15-ounce can black beans, rinsed and drained

1 1/2 cups cooked brown basmati rice, warm

1 large egg, beaten

1 tablespoon extra virgin olive oil, plus more for the skillet

1 garlic clove, minced

2 tablespoons very thinly sliced scallions (green onions)

1 tablespoon minced fresh flat-leaf parsley leaves

1/2 teaspoon kosher salt

1/2 teaspoon ground cumin

1/4 teaspoon cayenne pepper

Lettuce leaves, for serving

Your choice of slaw (pages 12 to 14), for serving (see Carla's Tips)

1 Grind 1 hamburger bun in a blender or food processor until fine crumbs form. Transfer 3/4 cup to a large bowl; reserve any remaining crumbs for another use. Toast the remaining buns and slather both cut sides with mayo.

2 To the bowl, add the beans, rice, egg, oil, garlic, scallions, parsley, salt, cumin, and cayenne. Use your fingers to mash it all up until the mixture comes together. The best kitchen tool is the one you're born with! Form the mixture into 4 patties the same diameter as your buns.

3 Lightly coat a large nonstick skillet with oil and heat it over medium heat. Add 2 patties and cook, turning once, until golden brown and heated through, about 4 minutes per side. Place lettuce leaves on your bottom buns and put the patties on top. Repeat with the remaining patties. Top the patties with slaw and the top buns.

• •

Carla's Tips

• Serve these with Creamy Cabbage Slaw or Tangy Hot Cabbage Slaw (pages 12 and 14) or any American-style slaw. If you choose a mayonnaise-y slaw, you don't need to spread any mayo on the buns.

• •

Turnovers, Pies & Tarts

A vegetarian main course can be as impressive as a meaty one, especially if it involves savory pastry. The combination of beautiful crust and super-tasty filling is so satisfying, and it looks good as a centerpiece. Pastry does require extra effort, but I think that's what makes it perfect for a vegetarian meal. It shows that it's worth spending the extra time to create a true main course for a meatless meal.

UNIVERSAL

Cream Cheese Dough
Makes enough for 8 large empanadas or samosas

Talk about a workhorse. This super easy dough was always my go-to in catering. It's a tender, not flaky, pastry. You basically can't overwork it, which would make it tough; it tastes great with both sweet and savory fillings; and it rolls out like a dream. If you've been scared to try making your own pastry, start here.

1 cup all-purpose flour

¹/₂ teaspoon salt

6 tablespoons (³/₄ stick) cold unsalted butter, cut into ¹/₂-inch dice

4 ounces cold cream cheese, cut into 1-inch dice

1 In the bowl of an electric mixer, mix the flour and salt. With your hands, toss the butter and cream cheese in the flour mixture until each piece is lightly coated.

2 With the paddle, beat on low speed until the dough forms a loose mass around the paddle.

3 Gently pat the dough into a 1-inch-thick rectangle on a large sheet of plastic wrap. Wrap it tightly in plastic wrap and refrigerate until firm, about 3 hours, before rolling. You can refrigerate the dough for up to 1 day or freeze it for up to 3 months.

Curried Potato Samosas

Serves 4 (makes 8)

My husband, Matthew, loves samosas—so much so that he doesn't even order them anymore. He doesn't have to! As soon as he calls our go-to Indian restaurant, whoever answers the phone recognizes his voice immediately and greets him, "Oh! Mr. Matt! Same order? Samosas?" Yes and yes. As much as he enjoys those samosas, I know he likes these homemade ones even more.

All-purpose flour, for rolling

Cream Cheese Dough (opposite)

2 cups Curried Potatoes and Peas (page 80)

1 large egg

1 tablespoon water

1 Preheat the oven to 400°F. Line a baking sheet with parchment paper.

2 On a lightly floured surface and using a lightly floured rolling pin, roll the dough into a 20 by 10-inch rectangle. Cut the rectangle into eight 5-inch squares.

3 To form a samosa: Fold a dough square diagonally in half and pinch one side to seal it. Hold the resulting cone upright, with the open side up. Use a narrow spoon to scoop and press ¼ cup curried potatoes into the opening, then seal the open side. Set the samosa upright on the baking sheet, like a pyramid. Repeat with the remaining dough and filling, spacing the samosas 2 inches apart.

4 In a small bowl, beat together the egg and water. Brush the egg wash all over the samosas, being sure to coat the seams.

5 Bake until golden brown and heated through, about 30 minutes. Serve hot, warm, or at room temperature.

Serve with Nectarine Chutney (page 64).

. . . .

Carla's Tips

• I learned this wrapping technique from David Rosengarten in his cookbook *It's All American Food*. I think it maximizes the amount of filling you can get in there. An easier way to wrap samosas is to place the filling in one corner of the square, fold the dough over to enclose it, and then pinch the edges to seal them. Sit the wrapped samosas up on one side to replicate the same shape. You can't get quite as much filling in there, though, so don't try to use the whole ¼ cup.

. . . .

MEXICAN

Black Bean Empanadas

Serves 4 (makes 8)

Moving to Washington, D.C., for college was a great way for me to experience a lot of firsts—especially in food. I had my first empanadas when my friends took me on a late-night run to Julia's Empanadas. I kept going back after that and eventually made my own when I was catering. Julia made a bunch of fillings, but I stuck to black beans—they're so silky and creamy and they can take flavors so well. That's important in an empanada because anything you put in the shell needs to be extra flavorful. The dough is delicious, but you need a filling that can stand up to it. That's why I use sweet-savory picadillo mixed with cheese. These make a filling main dish, but you can also make them small to serve as appetizers.

All-purpose flour, for rolling

Cream Cheese Dough (page 164)

1 cup Black Bean Picadillo (page 160), preferably chilled

1 Preheat the oven to 400°F. Line a baking sheet with parchment paper.

2 On a lightly floured surface and using a lightly floured rolling pin, roll the dough to ⅛-inch thickness. Use a lightly floured 5-inch round cookie cutter to cut out 5 rounds. Gather the scraps, reroll, and cut out 3 more rounds.

3 To form an empanada: Put 2 tablespoons of the picadillo in the center of a dough round. Fold the dough over to enclose the filling and form a half-moon. Pinch the edges together to seal them, and create a ½-inch rim. Pinch one corner between your thumb and forefinger and fold it over the rim. Pinch the dough next to the fold and fold again. Continue pinching and folding to create a decorative rope rim. Repeat with the remaining dough and filling.

4 Transfer the empanadas to the baking sheet, spacing them 2 inches apart. Bake until golden brown and heated through, about 30 minutes. Let cool on the pan and serve hot, warm, or at room temperature.

Serve with Tangy Hot Cabbage Slaw (page 14).

• •

Carla's Tips

• If you want your empanadas to have a glossy top, brush with an egg wash before baking. When I did that, though, I found the crust wasn't as crisp. I much prefer a rustic look if it means I get a nicely browned crust.

• •

Butternut Squash Tarte Tatin

Serves 6

Years of experience in the kitchen have taught me that certain things should just work. That's a skill I really value now that I need to come up with lots of recipes every day for The Chew. *Last fall, I wanted to make a hearty savory autumnal tart that still had a hint of sweetness. Butternut squash can be as sweet and solid as the apples used in a traditional tarte tatin and holds up beautifully when flipped out of a skillet. Plus, it slices like a dream. This is the kind of pretty dish that looks like it takes more effort than it really does. If you've ever searched for a Thanksgiving main dish that can rival turkey, you've come to the right recipe.*

All-purpose flour, for rolling

1 round Carla's Crust (page 178)

One 4¹⁄₄-pound butternut squash, peeled, cut in half lengthwise, seeded, and cut into ¹⁄₄-inch-thick slices

1 medium yellow onion, cut in half and thinly sliced

3 garlic cloves, sliced

2 tablespoons extra virgin olive oil

Kosher salt and freshly ground black pepper

2 tablespoons unsalted butter

2 tablespoons fresh lemon juice

1¹⁄₂ tablespoons honey

1 teaspoon freshly grated lemon zest, plus more for garnish

1¹⁄₂ teaspoons fresh thyme leaves, plus more for garnish

1 teaspoon chopped fresh sage leaves, plus more for garnish

1 Preheat the oven to 400°F. Line a baking sheet with parchment paper.

2 On a lightly floured surface and using a lightly floured rolling pin, roll the dough into a 10-inch round. Transfer it to the baking sheet and refrigerate.

3 In a large bowl, toss the butternut squash, onion, garlic, oil, 1 teaspoon salt, and ¹⁄₂ teaspoon pepper. Divide between two rimmed baking sheets and spread out evenly.

4 Bake until the squash is lightly browned and still slightly firm to the touch, about 25 minutes. Cool slightly on wire racks. Turn the oven down to 375°F.

5 In a 9-inch cast-iron skillet, melt the butter over medium heat. Add the lemon juice and honey and stir until bubbly. Remove from the heat and stir in the lemon zest, thyme, sage, and a pinch each of salt and pepper.

(continued on next page)

6 Layer the roasted squash over the honey in concentric circles, stacking the layers all the way to the top of the pan. Make the first layer extra pretty because the pan will be inverted and the bottom will be presented as the top. Center the pastry round on top, tucking the edges in loosely.

7 Bake until the crust is light golden brown, about 30 minutes. Cool on a wire rack for 15 minutes, then very carefully invert onto a platter. Garnish with lemon zest, thyme, and sage.

Carla's Tips

• Choose a platter with a diameter that's slightly larger than the skillet. It should be flat but have a slight rim to keep any juices in.

• The easiest way to flip out a tarte tatin is to invert the platter over the skillet. Wearing oven mitts, use both hands to securely hold the skillet and the platter together, and swiftly flip them over. Carefully lower the whole thing onto your counter, then lift off the skillet. Be very careful! Don't burn yourself!

Spanakopita: Lemon-Scented Spinach and Feta Pie

Serves 12

Every Greek restaurant has a version of this savory greens and cheese pie. My little twist is to spike the mixture with lemon zest; it adds a level of freshness. I experimented with this dish many times, trying to prevent the filo from getting soggy by the time the whole thing cools, and this recipe comes pretty close. I switched from a cake pan to a shallow one, added an egg to the filling, drained the cheese, and squeezed every last drop of liquid out of the spinach. The real secret, though, is to eat it when it's still hot so the top is all shattery, the center creamy, and the bottom crisp.

Olive oil cooking spray

2 tablespoons extra virgin olive oil

1 bunch scallions (green onions), trimmed and thinly sliced

1 large shallot, finely chopped

2 garlic cloves, minced

Kosher salt

2 pounds baby spinach

1/2 cup fresh flat-leaf parsley leaves, finely chopped

1 large egg, beaten

1 cup crumbled feta cheese

1/2 cup ricotta cheese, drained

1 tablespoon freshly grated lemon zest

1/4 teaspoon freshly grated nutmeg

Ten 18 by 13-inch sheets filo dough, thawed if frozen

1 Preheat the oven to 350°F. Lightly coat a 13 by 9 by 1-inch baking pan with olive oil spray.

2 Heat the oil in a large, deep skillet over medium heat. Add the scallions, shallot, garlic, and a pinch of salt. Cook, stirring frequently, until softened and lightly browned, about 5 minutes. Stir in the spinach, parsley, and pinch of salt. Cook, stirring, until the spinach wilts, about 2 minutes. Drain in a fine-mesh colander, squeezing the spinach as dry as possible. Finely chop the spinach.

3 In a large bowl, stir together the egg, feta, ricotta, lemon zest, and nutmeg until smooth. Stir in the spinach mixture until well blended.

4 Lay 1 filo sheet in the prepared pan, aligning one short edge with the length of the pan. Spray the sheet, then fold it in half so that it covers the bottom of the pan. Repeat laying, spraying, and folding 4 times so that you've used 5 filo sheets total, forming 10 layers. Spread the spinach evenly over the filo stack. Then repeat the laying, spraying, and folding with the remaining 5 filo sheets.

(continued on next page)

5 Fold any overhanging edges of filo over the filling. Use an offset spatula to tightly tuck the folded edges against the filling by placing the spatula's edge where the ends of the sheets meet the edge of the pan and gently pressing the sheets toward the bottom of the pan. Repeat all around the perimeter of the pan to encase the filling. Coat the top with the oil spray.

6 Bake until golden brown, about 40 minutes. Cool slightly in the pan on a rack, then cut into pieces and serve hot.

Carla's Tips

• You may not be able to fit all the spinach into the skillet at once. If you can't, add half and stir until it wilts, then add the rest. It's amazing how such a huge amount of spinach will shrink!

• Be sure to squeeze the spinach dry before layering it. If it's too wet, it'll make the filo soggy.

Turning Out Turnovers

I like to tell people I'm a recovering caterer. Other caterers know exactly what I mean by that. Regular folks have no idea. The first time I did spanakopita for a client? I'm still recovering from that—over fifteen years later. It was a Fourth of July blowout in Rehoboth, Delaware, far enough from D.C. that I had to go the day before and spend the night there. Carrie, a young woman I borrowed from another caterer, suggested I make lemon-scented spanakopita for the party. She knew I loved lemon and these small savory pastries seemed like an ideal finger food for our guests. I said, "Great! Let's do it!"

Here's how they're traditionally made: tissue-thin layers of delicate filo dough, which tears easily, are brushed with melted butter, then stacked, then folded into triangles around a spinach-feta filling. One by one, you brush, stack, fold. I was folding up those tiny triangles until the cows came home. Seeing the sun rise on Rehoboth Beach is pretty and all, but . . .

I knew there had to be a better way for home cooks. Over the years, I've toyed with the filling, lightening it with ricotta and egg, and, crucially, I've stopped doing the pastries as individual triangles. Now I make the whole thing in a pan, then cut it up. Honestly, they're a little messier to eat this way, but the flavors are still great. When you're cooking and entertaining at home, a little messy is totally fine. It makes guests feel comfortable, like family. You want perfect hors d'oeuvres to pick up with your fingers? Call a caterer.

Moussaka: Tomato-Eggplant Casserole

Serves 8

For years, I didn't do too much with eggplant. I had had enough of it when I started out at the Henley Park Hotel restaurant. I was the low man on the totem pole there, so every day, I had to really finely julienne eggplant skins and deep-fry and salt them for a pretty garnish. I've since recovered and can't get enough of this particular dish. My Chew *co-host Michael Symon made an amazing lamb version on the show. If you're a regular viewer of* The Chew, *you'll know that it was Michael's moussaka that I stole from the staff fridge! Oops! I couldn't get enough of it! I figured I'd better make my own and decided to make the eggplant the star of the dish. I ditched the meat for hearty quick-cooking bulgur, which adds a satisfying chew to the mix and makes this filling enough to be a main course.*

4 tablespoons extra virgin olive oil

Kosher salt

3 large globe eggplants, trimmed, peeled, and cut into 1-inch-thick rounds

1 large yellow onion, diced

4 garlic cloves, chopped

1/4 teaspoon ground allspice

1/4 teaspoon ground cinnamon

1/8 teaspoon ground cloves

1/2 cup bulgur

One 14.5-ounce can diced fire-roasted tomatoes

2 teaspoons chopped fresh oregano leaves

2 cups Vegetable Stock (page 103) or store-bought unsalted vegetable broth

1/2 cup ricotta cheese

1/2 cup plain whole-milk Greek yogurt

1/4 cup freshly grated Parmigiano-Reggiano cheese

3 large eggs, beaten

1/8 teaspoon freshly grated nutmeg

1 Arrange the broiler rack 6 inches from the heat source. Preheat the broiler.

2 Brush a rimmed baking sheet with 1 tablespoon of the oil and sprinkle ½ teaspoon salt over it. Arrange the eggplant slices in a single layer in the pan, then brush the tops with 2 tablespoons oil and sprinkle with ½ teaspoon salt.

3 Broil, turning once, until both sides are nicely browned, about 15 minutes. Remove the eggplant and turn the oven to 350°F.

4 Heat the remaining 1 tablespoon oil in a large skillet over medium-low heat. Add the onion and 1 teaspoon salt. Cook, stirring occasionally, until translucent, about 5 minutes. Add the garlic, allspice, cinnamon, and cloves and cook, stirring, for 1 minute. Add the bulgur and cook, stirring, for 1 minute.

5 Stir in the tomatoes with their juices, oregano, and stock. Bring to a boil, then reduce the heat and simmer for 20 minutes.

6 Meanwhile, in a large bowl, stir the ricotta, yogurt, Parmigiano-Reggiano, eggs, nutmeg, ½ teaspoon salt, and ¼ teaspoon pepper until well mixed.

7 To assemble the moussaka: Spread a third of the tomato sauce in a shallow 3-quart baking dish. Arrange half of the eggplant on top, overlapping the slices slightly. Repeat the layers and then spread the remaining sauce on top. Dollop the ricotta mixture over the sauce and gently spread it to cover the top.

8 Bake until the top is golden and the liquid bubbling, about 35 minutes. Let cool slightly before serving.

Desserts

I love baking. Even though I came to it late in life, I knew I had found my calling once I did. That's why I started a cookie company and why I spend so much of my time thinking about what I can do with sugar, butter, flour, and every other ingredient in the world. Chances are, if I'm staring off into the distance, I'm thinking about a new dessert.

Yet, I don't have an intense sweet tooth. I love treats, but I go light on the sugar. I add enough to make the treat yummy, but not so much that it masks the other good stuff goin' on. If you prefer sweeter treats, I tell you where you can go at it in these recipes.

• •

Pastries

Baking anything that combines crust with yummy filling makes me so happy. The pairing can come in many forms and still be beautiful and delicious, no matter how different. A tart can have a perfectly even, fluted edge and decorative top and be just the thing for a fancy party. A pie can be rustic and lumpy and look awesome on the picnic table. For this collection, I did a range of shapes and sizes and styles and I could eat every one of them all day long.

Left: Quince Corn Cake (recipe page 209)

Carla's Crust

Makes two 9 by 13-inch cobbler crusts or
two 9-inch round pie crusts

*For more years than I can count, I've been making
this flaky, tender, all-butter crust. It's my go-to, and
the technique has been perfected through years of
mixing and rolling.*

1 tablespoon sugar

1 teaspoon table salt

⅓ cup cold water

2 cups all-purpose flour

**½ pound (2 sticks) cold unsalted butter,
cut into ½-inch dice**

1 Chill the bowl and paddle attachment of a standing electric mixer until cold. In a small bowl, dissolve the sugar and salt in the water, and chill until
cold.

2 In the chilled mixer bowl, combine the flour
and butter and toss until the butter pieces are
well coated. Mix with the paddle on low speed until
the butter forms pea-size pieces. Add the water
mixture all at once, increase the speed to medium,
and beat just until the dough comes together.

3 Flatten the dough into two 1-inch-thick rectan-
gles for cobbler crusts or two 1-inch-thick disks
for pies. Wrap the dough tightly in plastic wrap and
chill until firm, at least 30 minutes or up to 1 day.
(You can also freeze the dough for up to 3 months.
Thaw in the refrigerator or at room temperature.)

Less Is More

Whenever Granny had the whole family over to dinner, she baked my favorite dessert: peach cobbler. She'd start by cooking down soft peaches so that they'd caramelize into the buttery dough. In the oven, the crust would go deep brown and the peaches would cling to it, creating a sticky brick-red sheen. Granny would make it in whichever tin she had lyin' around: a dented square one, an old round one. Putting the cobbler together was second nature to her and the smell of it was heaven.

There was only one problem: She never made enough! No matter what she baked it in, the container never seemed big enough. Sure, we could all have one serving, but I wanted seconds. I always wanted to say, "Granny! You knew we were all coming! Why didn't you make more?"

The answer was right in front of my face. Granny always did make more ... of other dishes. She wanted us to have a little taste of everything and I wanted to stuff my pie hole with cobbler.

Now I wonder, too, whether she was showing us love with her food by giving us the right amount of it. We never ever went hungry at her house, but we never left uncomfortably stuffed either. Granny didn't skimp on flavor or even on fat, but she was conscious of what she put in her dishes.

I've taken that lesson from Granny and applied it to my own life, especially since my life revolves around eating. I actually enjoy my food more, and especially my sweets, when I get smaller tastes of them. I fully appreciate their nuances then and am satisfied with having a little treat. So maybe I won't take seconds of that cobbler, but I am definitely baking mine in a bigger pan . . .

 SOUTHERN

Peach Cobbler

Serves 12

When I moved up north, I was so confused by cobbler. Every time I ordered it, I'd get this thing with drops of biscuit dough or some sort of cakey batter baked on top of the fruit. That's certainly not the cobbler I knew in Granny's kitchen. Granny, and many Southern home cooks like her, did peach cobbler with a pie crust on top and bottom. It's not the same as a double-crust pie because the sides are open to let the juices run all over. I've keep the spirit of Granny's with a buttery crust, but now I bake the bottom crust before adding the filling to keep it crisp. And instead of simmering the fruit to a jammy state on the stovetop, I roast it to intensify its sweetness while keeping the shapes of the slices. Aside from those little touches, this is a taste of a true Southern cobbler.

All-purpose flour, for rolling

Carla's Crust (page 178)

8 ripe but firm yellow peaches, peeled, pitted, and cut into ½-inch-thick slices

¼ cup granulated sugar

¼ cup packed light or dark brown sugar

¼ teaspoon ground cinnamon

¼ teaspoon freshly grated nutmeg

1 teaspoon fresh lemon juice

2 teaspoons amaretto liqueur

1 tablespoon cornstarch

Pinch of table salt

1 large egg

1 tablespoon water

**1 tablespoon coarse sugar
(see Carla's Tips)**

1 Preheat the oven to 425°F. Line two rimmed baking sheets with parchment paper.

2 Lightly dust your work surface and rolling pin with flour. Swirl one dough rectangle in the flour to lightly coat the bottom (you want to make sure the dough can move while you're rolling it out). Roll the rectangle from the center out, then rotate it a quarter turn and roll again. Keep rolling and turning to form a 13 by 9-inch rectangle, lightly, lightly flouring the surface and the top of the dough as you work. You want just enough flour to keep the dough from sticking; don't overflour! Transfer the dough to one of the baking sheets, and refrigerate.

3 Repeat the rolling out with the other piece of dough. Place it on the second baking sheet and bake until golden brown, about 20 minutes. Cool completely on the baking sheet on a wire rack. Meanwhile, turn the oven down to 375°F.

4 While the dough is cooling, make the filling: On another rimmed baking sheet or in a shallow baking dish, combine the peaches, sugars, cinnamon, nutmeg, lemon juice, amaretto, cornstarch, and salt, tossing until well mixed. Roast in the oven until the fruit releases its juices, about 20 minutes.

5 In a small bowl, beat the egg with the water. Transfer the cooled baked crust to a shallow 13 by 9-inch baking dish and spread the hot peach filling evenly over the crust. Top with the chilled unbaked dough, brush with the egg wash, and sprinkle with the coarse sugar.

6 Bake until the crust is golden and the fruit is bubbling, about 1 hour and 20 minutes. Let cool slightly and serve warm.

· ·

• **Swap Out:** If you don't have coarse sugar, sprinkle granulated on top.

• **Sweet Tooth:** Serve with ice cream or sweetened whipped cream.

· ·

Rustic Bacon-Apple Pie

Makes two 9-inch pies

When I finished my runs on Top Chef, *I told myself, "No regrets. You did your best, made it to the finals, and won fan favorite! No regrets." I never thought about going back to my time on the show to figure out how I'd do things differently . . . until I thought about apple pie. I make a good pie. It's one of my things. When we were faced with a pie competition on* Top Chef, *I should've won it, easy. But I made this great apple pie, then (stupidly!) stuck a slice of cheddar on the side. It sat there on the edge of the plate, looking like a neglected stepchild. A slice of cheese on apple pie's a traditional pairing in parts of the country, but my version didn't come together. Fast forward to* The Chew: *my co-host Mario Batali suggested I try doing a pie crust with cheddar . . . and bacon. As soon as he said it, I knew I had to do it. When I did, I was wowed by the savory, super-rich crust that was so perfect for apples. This pie right here, this would've won* Top Chef.

2 teaspoons cornstarch

1 teaspoon vanilla extract

1/4 cup plus 1 tablespoon water

1 tablespoon unsalted butter

1 teaspoon canola oil

6 apples, a mix of tart and sweet, such as Granny Smith and Golden Delicious, cut into quarters, cored, and thinly sliced crosswise

1/3 cup packed light or dark brown sugar

1 teaspoon fresh lemon juice

1/2 teaspoon kosher salt

All-purpose flour, for rolling

Cheddar Bacon Crust (page 185)

1 large egg, beaten

2 tablespoons coarse sugar

1 In a small bowl, stir together the cornstarch, vanilla, and 1/4 cup water until smooth.

2 In a very large skillet, melt the butter in the oil over medium-high heat. Add the apples and cook, tossing and stirring occasionally, until lightly charred, about 5 minutes.

3 Add the brown sugar, lemon juice, and salt. Cook, stirring frequently, until the sugar dissolves, about 2 minutes. Add the cornstarch mixture and cook, stirring, until the liquid thickens, about 1 minute. Remove from the heat and let cool completely.

4 Preheat the oven to 375°F. Line a large rimmed baking sheet with parchment paper.

(continued on next page)

5 On a lightly floured surface and using a lightly floured rolling pin, roll each piece of dough into a ¼-inch-thick round. Transfer to the prepared baking sheet. Divide the cooled filling between the two rounds, leaving a 2-inch border. Fold and pleat the border up and around the apples, leaving the center open.

6 In a small bowl, beat the remaining 1 tablespoon water into the egg. Brush the egg wash over the dough, and sprinkle with the coarse sugar. Bake until the crust is golden brown, about 45 minutes. Cool completely on a wire rack.

Carla's Tips

• When my co-author, Genevieve, and I were making this recipe, we each took a round of dough to roll and shape the pies. I piled my apples into a dome and gathered the dough high up around them; she spread her apples into an even layer and folded the dough flat over them. It was fun to see how we instinctively shaped our rustic pies differently, even though our dough rounds were the same shape and size and we had equal amounts of apple. My tall pie baked up into soft apples in a tender crust; her pie turned into toothsome apples in a crisp crust. I love both styles! Try one of each or create your own rustic pie style.

• **Swap Out:** If you don't have coarse sugar, sprinkle granulated on top.

• **Sweet Tooth:** Sprinkle sugar over the apples before baking, then serve with a scoop of ice cream.

 ALL-AMERICAN

Cheddar Bacon Crust

Makes two 9-inch pie crusts

This crust would also be good in savory quiches and pies, or rolled, cut, baked, and eaten as a savory cookie or shortbread.

¹/₂ **teaspoon kosher salt**

¹/₃ **cup cold water**

2 ounces thick-cut bacon, finely diced and frozen

2 cups all-purpose flour

2 ounces sharp cheddar cheese, grated (¹/₂ cup) and chilled

8 tablespoons (1 stick) unsalted butter, cut into ¹/₄-inch-thick slices and chilled

1 In a small bowl, stir the salt into the cold water until it dissolves.

2 In the bowl of a food processor, use your hands to toss the bacon with the flour until well coated. (Watch out for the blade!) Pulse until coarse crumbs form. Transfer to a large bowl.

3 Toss the cheese and butter into the flour mixture, and then press in the butter with your fingertips until coarse crumbs form with a few bigger pieces remaining. Add the salted water all at once, and quickly gather the dough with your hands into a large, shaggy clump.

4 Divide the dough into 2 equal pieces, shape into disks, cover tightly with plastic wrap, and chill until firm, at least 1 hour and up to 3 days.

• •

Carla's Tips

• If you want to bake this crust into savory cookies, roll out the dough until ¹/₄-inch thick, cut out the shapes you'd like, and bake on parchment-lined baking sheets in a 350°F oven until golden brown. If you want a sweeter cookie, brush the dough shapes with a little egg wash and coat the tops with coarse sugar before baking.

• •

 ALL-AMERICAN

Pear-Cranberry Pot Pie

Serves 10

Savory cooking techniques often sneak into my sweet baking. I approached this recipe the way I do my chicken pot pie: I cooked the filling first, then tossed it with a sauce, then sandwiched the hot stuff between fully baked crisp crusts. To make this fall sweet extra-special for a Thanksgiving feast, I put walnuts into my crust, making it super buttery and flaky. What I love most about this dish is how each component works great on its own or in other applications (think ice cream). As a trio, they're amazing.

8 large ripe but firm Bosc pears, peeled, cored, and cut into ³/₄-inch chunks

¹/₂ teaspoon freshly grated nutmeg

¹/₂ teaspoon kosher salt

¹/₂ cup plus 2 tablespoons packed light brown sugar

2 tablespoons canola oil

1¹/₂ teaspoons ground cinnamon

1¹/₂ cups fresh or thawed frozen cranberries

Cranberry Apple Syrup (recipe follows), warmed

20 Flaky Walnut Cookies (page 197)

1 Preheat the oven to 425°F. On a rimmed baking sheet, toss the pears, nutmeg, salt, ¹/₂ cup brown sugar, 1 tablespoon of the oil, and 1 teaspoon of the cinnamon until well mixed. Spread out in a single layer and roast until the pears are golden and crisp-tender, about 40 minutes.

2 Meanwhile, on another baking sheet, toss the cranberries, remaining 2 tablespoons brown sugar, remaining 1 tablespoon oil, and remaining ¹/₂ teaspoon cinnamon until well mixed. Roast alongside the pears until the berries have burst, about 10 minutes.

3 Transfer the cranberries to a large bowl, add the pears when they are done, and stir in the warm syrup.

4 Divide 10 walnut cookies among individual serving dishes, and top each with the syrupy fruit and another cookie.

• •

Carla's Tips

• I prefer to cut the fruit in chunks instead of slices because slices break down too much for this to taste like a pot pie. Texture's what I'm after in the filling, and I love the fruit when it's tender but still has some chew.

• You can definitely do this pot pie with apples, or a mix of apples and pears. I love baking with firm Bosc pears even though they're not the tastiest raw. With pears, the best ones for eating aren't necessarily the best ones for baking. Apples are another story. I like to bake with a variety of sweet and tart apples, such as Fuji and Pink Lady. Since you can buy apples separately at the market anyway, you might as well choose lots of different kinds!

• **Sweet Tooth:** Scoop some ice cream on top.

• •

Cranberry Apple Syrup

Makes about 1¹/₂ cups

The natural sweetness in fruit has such an amazing complexity. One of my go-to tricks is to make a syrup by reducing no-sugar-added store-bought juices until most of their water evaporates. Spices add a great kick and a little cornstarch gives the sauce body.

1¹/₂ cups pure unsweetened cranberry juice

1¹/₂ cups fresh unsweetened apple cider

1 cinnamon stick

One 1-inch piece fresh ginger, peeled and sliced

¹/₂ teaspoon freshly grated nutmeg

2 strips lemon zest, removed with a vegetable peeler

¹/₂ cup packed light brown sugar

1 tablespoon cornstarch

1 tablespoon cold water

1 In a large saucepan, bring the cranberry juice, apple cider, cinnamon stick, ginger, nutmeg, lemon zest, and brown sugar to a boil over high heat, stirring occasionally. Boil until reduced by half, about 20 minutes. Strain through a sieve, return the liquid to the saucepan, and discard the solids.

2 In a small bowl, stir the cornstarch into the cold water until dissolved.

3 Bring the strained juices to a steady simmer, and then whisk in the cornstarch slurry. Simmer until thickened slightly, about 10 minutes.

• •

Carla's Tips

• Use this syrup in cocktails or tea, over ice cream, with roasted or poached fruits, on pound cake, pancakes, waffles, French toast . . . the possibilities are endless!

• **Sweet Tooth:** Add more sugar to the simmering mixture or start with sweetened cranberry juice.

• •

GREEK

Baklava

Makes 40 large pieces

For years, I've been ordering baklava for dessert every time I get dinner from The Big Greek Café, a neighborhood joint near my home in D.C. I've always enjoyed theirs as much as the buttery one I made for catering. Then I tried my friend Gail's version. She's a vegan caterer who worked in the kitchen space next to mine when I was still catering. Her baklava was the best I ever had and it completely changed my view on what baklava's all about. I thought the buttered layers made the dessert. Turns out olive oil adds more complex flavors and highlights the richness of the nuts. As a bonus, olive oil spray makes this labor-intensive dessert go much faster than brushing with butter. I've kept a touch of creamy butter here and I think the balance is just right.

2¹/₂ cups walnut halves, finely chopped

2 cups slivered almonds, finely chopped

1¹/₂ cups shelled pistachios, finely chopped

3 tablespoons sugar

2 teaspoons ground cinnamon

¹/₂ teaspoon ground cardamom

¹/₂ teaspoon ground ginger

¹/₂ teaspoon table salt

4 tablespoons (¹/₂ stick) unsalted butter, melted, or extra virgin olive oil

One 1-pound package filo dough (18 by 13-inch sheets), thawed if frozen

Olive oil cooking spray

Spiced Citrus Simple Syrup (recipe follows)

1 Preheat the oven to 350°F. In a large bowl, combine the walnuts, almonds, pistachios, sugar, cinnamon, cardamom, ginger, and salt.

2 It's time to assemble the baklava! You need to work quickly, so be sure to have everything in place: rimmed baking sheet, melted butter and brush, filo covered with a clean kitchen towel to prevent drying, olive oil spray, bowl of nuts with a cup measure for scooping.

3 Brush the baking sheet with 2 tablespoons of the butter. Lay 1 filo sheet in the pan, generously coat with olive oil spray, and top with another sheet. Repeat to make a stack of 8 sheets. Cover the remaining filo to prevent it from drying out. Spread 2 cups of the nuts evenly over the filo stack. Lay a filo sheet on top, spray, lay another sheet, and spray. Spread 2 cups nuts over the filo. Repeat: 2 sheets sprayed filo, then top with the remaining 2 cups nuts. Cover the remaining filo with the kitchen towel.

4 Fold any overhanging edges of filo over the nut filling. Use an offset spatula to tightly tuck the folded edges against the filling by placing the spatula's edge where the ends of the sheets meet the edge of the pan and gently pressing the sheets toward the bottom of the pan. Repeat all around the perimeter of the pan. (You need to encase the filling to prevent the soaking syrup from spilling out later.) Coat the top with olive oil spray and lay a filo sheet on top. Repeat 7 times to make a topping with 8 sheets total. You don't need to tuck these edges in. Brush the remaining 2 tablespoons butter on top, using small brushing motions to prevent the filo from crinkling.

5 Use a very sharp knife (preferably serrated) to cut the whole pan of baklava in half crosswise, then into quarters, then eighths to form 8 short, even rows, cutting almost all the way through to the pan. Use small sawing strokes to prevent the filo from dragging with your knife, and hold the filo down around your cuts to keep it in place. Then, starting from a corner, cut diagonally to meet the opposite edge of the pan, ending at the intersection of a crosswise cut. Move to the corner of the next row and cut a line parallel to the first to meet the opposite edge of the pan. You will have formed a diagonal row of trapezoids with triangles at the ends. Continue cutting from corners to edges until half of the pan has been cut. Rotate the pan 180 degrees and repeat the cutting from the other side until the whole pan has been cut.

6 Bake until golden brown, about 40 minutes. Transfer the pan to a cooling rack, and immediately and slowly pour the syrup all over the baklava. Be sure to get syrup into every row. Let sit for at least 3 hours, then serve.

Spiced Citrus Simple Syrup

Makes about 2 cups

Citrus makes everything better. This simple syrup's meant for baklava, but it's also perfect for yogurt, fruit, or a hot cup of tea. Choose a honey that you like here, but be sure to stick with something relatively mild, like orange blossom or wildflower.

1½ cups sugar

1½ cups water

½ cup honey

Finely grated zest of 1 orange

1 strip lemon zest, removed with a vegetable peeler

1 tablespoon fresh lemon juice

1 cinnamon stick

1 cardamom pod

1 In a small saucepan, bring the sugar, water, honey, orange zest, lemon zest and juice, cinnamon stick, and cardamom pod to a boil, stirring to dissolve the sugar. Boil for 1 minute, then remove from the heat. Let cool to room temperature.

2 Strain through a fine-mesh sieve and discard the solids. The syrup can be refrigerated in an airtight container for up to 1 week.

• •

Carla's Tips

• If you happen to have made the Persian Jeweled Rice (page 73) for dinner, swap that simple syrup for the sugar and water here and bring to a boil with the remaining ingredients. Steep until room temperature, then strain.

• •

Simple Secrets to Perfect Baklava

- Start 6 to 8 hours before you want to serve this. It requires a little planning, but that makes it the best make-ahead dessert.

- To make this vegan, buy vegan filo and use only olive oil.

- You'll need a whole 5-ounce can of spray. If you don't want to use spray, brush the oil on instead.

- If you're all about the butter, do this with clarified butter. Brush in small, short strokes with a natural-bristle pastry brush. You'll need at least a pound of butter for this recipe.

- Use a pan that you don't mind getting cut marks. Make sure it's a heavy baking sheet.

- You only need one box of filo, but start with two if you've never made baklava before.

- Filo is pennies to a sheet, so if a piece tears or just isn't working, ball it up and throw it away. Don't waste your energy trying to fix it. Take a deep breath and move on to the next sheet.

- I like the proportions of the different types of nuts here, but do what you like as long as you end up with 6 cups total.

- Taste your nuts before starting. You do not want any rancid ones to ruin your beautiful dessert.

- It takes a long time to chop all the nuts, but you get great texture that way. If you're in a rush, you can pulse the nuts in a food processor, but they won't chop as evenly and you'll end up with powdery nuts and possibly paste. Don't say I didn't warn you!

- A bread knife or serrated knife cuts through the layers easily.

- Leftovers freeze well. Wrap them tightly in plastic wrap and freeze for up to 1 month. Simply thaw before serving.

 ALL-AMERICAN

Salted Peanut Chocolate Pudding Tarts

Serves 8

A few years ago, I felt so honored when I was asked to make dessert for the James Beard Award winners at their annual gala. I decided to do chocolate pudding tarts in a pecan shortbread crust. It was such a hit that I knew it'd be just as good, if not better, in a salted peanut crust. The secret to my technique is to fully bake the crusts, then fill them with warm pudding. This allows the top of the pudding filling to set evenly with no effort and it melds the flavors together. Each bite takes you from crunchy nut top to silky ganache to creamy pudding and back to crunchy nut. This tart captures my spirit as a baker: It's all elegance with a down-home flavor that hits that happy, nostalgic sweet spot.

3 tablespoons cornstarch

²/₃ cup sugar

2 tablespoons plus 1 teaspoon
  unsweetened cocoa powder

¹/₂ teaspoon table salt

2 ²/₃ cups whole milk

1 cup heavy cream

3 ounces bittersweet (70%) chocolate,
  melted

2 ounces high-quality milk (41%)
  chocolate, melted

4 large egg yolks

2 tablespoons unsalted butter, at room
  temperature

2 teaspoons vanilla extract

Salted Peanut Shortbread (page 195),
  baked into eight 4-inch tart shells

Milk Chocolate Ganache (recipe follows),
  warm

¹/₂ cup chopped roasted salted peanuts

1 In a large saucepan, whisk the cornstarch, sugar, cocoa powder, and salt. Gradually whisk in the milk and cream, and bring to a low boil over medium-low heat. Remove from the heat and whisk in the two melted chocolates. Continue whisking until smooth.

2 In a large bowl, whisk the egg yolks until broken. Very gradually add a little of the hot milk mixture to the yolks, whisking continuously. When the bottom of the mixing bowl is warm, whisk in the remaining hot milk.

3 Pour the mixture back into the saucepan and cook over medium-low heat, stirring continuously. Be sure to scrape along the bottom and sides of the pan. Continue cooking and stirring until the pudding thickens, increasing the speed of your stirring as the custard gets thicker, about 10 minutes. You want to actually boil the custard but not burn it, so keep stirring while it bubbles and gets really thick. Let it boil for 30 seconds, then remove from the heat.

(continued on next page)

4 Strain the pudding through a fine-mesh sieve into a large bowl. Fold in the butter and vanilla until fully incorporated. Divide among the tart shells and refrigerate, uncovered, until firm and set, at least 4 hours and up to overnight.

5 Divide the warm ganache among the tarts, swirling to evenly coat the tops. Sprinkle 1 table-spoon of the peanuts on top of each tart. Refriger-ate, uncovered, until set, at least 10 minutes and up to 1 day.

Carla's Tips

• Try to find smaller peanuts; they're crunchier and less greasy than the big cocktail ones.

Milk Chocolate Ganache

Makes about 1 cup

Good milk chocolate is really good: silky and creamy with caramel undertones. Please, please use it here. This just won't taste right or set properly if you use a candy bar. Look for milk chocolate that's 35% to 45% cacao and bittersweet that's 65% to 75% cacao.

¹⁄₄ cup chopped milk chocolate

1 cup chopped bittersweet chocolate

1 cup heavy cream

Place the chocolate in a large bowl. Heat the cream in a small saucepan until bubbles form around the edge. Pour over the chocolate, then gently stir with a wooden spoon until smooth.

Carla's Tips

• If your chocolate doesn't melt all the way, whiz the ganache in a food processor until smooth.

Nut Cookies

I'm all about nuts in my cookies. When I started my cookie company, Carla Hall Petite Cookies, I knew I wanted the buttery richness of nuts in both my sweet and savory treats. They bring this awesome depth of flavor and subtle, natural sweetness, all while giving you a little something to crunch. To make my nut cookies extra tasty, I always make sure the nuts are fresh. I nibble ones I plan on using to know whether or not they're rancid. If you don't, you may end up having to dump a whole batch of freshly baked cookies! (I've been there.) Your best bet is to buy nuts just before you plan to use them from a store that keeps their inventory moving. If you're not using them right away, keep them in an airtight container in the freezer.

 ALL-AMERICAN

Salted Peanut Shortbread

Makes about 11 dozen cookie bites or eight 4-inch tart shells

I'd been dreaming of creating a line of these for my petite cookie company, but we're a peanut-free facility, so I never had a chance to make them there. In my home kitchen, however, I got to toy around and came up with these bites. First time around, they were fine. Second time, I sprinkled the tops with fleur de sel. When I popped one in my mouth, I knew I had nailed it. You still can't buy peanut shortbread from Carla Hall Petite Cookies but here you are, folks, your very own recipe for them.

2 cups roasted salted peanuts

1 cup all-purpose flour, plus more for rolling

¾ teaspoon table salt

8 tablespoons (1 stick) unsalted butter, at room temperature

¾ cup sugar

1 large egg yolk

2 teaspoons vanilla extract

Fleur de sel or other coarse salt, for sprinkling (optional)

1 In a food processor, pulse ¾ cup of the peanuts with ¼ cup of the flour and the salt until the peanuts are very finely ground. Transfer to a large bowl. Repeat with another ¾ cup peanuts and ¼ cup flour. Coarsely chop the remaining ½ cup peanuts and place them in another bowl.

2 In the bowl of an electric mixer fitted with the paddle, beat the butter and sugar on medium-high speed until creamy but still gritty, about 2 minutes. Beat in the egg yolk and vanilla. Reduce the

(continued on next page)

speed to low and beat in the remaining ½ cup flour, then the peanut flour, and finally the chopped peanuts.

3 Transfer the dough to a gallon-size heavy-duty resealable plastic bag and press it into a ½-inch-thick rectangle, squeezing the dough all the way to the bottom and sides of the bag. (The rectangle will be about 3 inches shy of the top.) Seal tightly and refrigerate until very firm, up to 1 day.

4 When ready to bake, preheat the oven to 350°F. Line several baking sheets with parchment paper if making cookies. Cut open the bag and peel off the dough.

5 *If making cookies:* Cut the dough into ½-inch dice. Place on the baking sheets, spacing them ½ inch apart. Sprinkle the tops of the cookies with a little fleur de sel if using. Bake until golden brown, about 15 minutes, rotating the sheets halfway through. Cool completely on the sheets on wire racks.

6 *If making tart shells:* Roll the dough between sheets of lightly floured parchment paper to an even ⅛-inch thickness. Use a 6-inch round cookie cutter to cut out rounds. Gather and reroll the scraps to cut more rounds; you should have 8 total. Carefully transfer the rounds to 4-inch round tart pans with removable bottoms, pressing the dough into the bottoms and up the sides. If necessary, trim the edge flush with the rim of the pan. Sprinkle with a little fleur de sel, if using. If the dough has softened, refrigerate again until firm. Prick the bottoms with a fork, then bake on a baking sheet until brown, about 15 minutes. Cool completely in the pans on a wire rack.

 ALL-AMERICAN

Flaky Walnut Cookies

Makes 20

Ever bake and eat your pie pastry scraps? So yummy, right? That's basically what these are, but the walnuts take them to another level. Sanded with sugar, they make amazing tender-flaky melt-in-your-mouth cookies. Baked plain, you can pair them with sweet fillings or savory cheese or use them in the Pear-Cranberry Pot Pie (page 186).

1 teaspoon kosher salt

1/3 cup plus 1 teaspoon cold water

1 cup walnuts

1 1/2 cups all-purpose flour, plus more
   for rolling

3 tablespoons sugar, plus more for
   sprinkling

12 tablespoons (1 1/2 sticks) cold unsalted
   butter, cut into thin pats

1 large egg white

1 In a small bowl, stir the salt and 1/3 cup cold water until the salt dissolves.

2 In a food processor, pulse the walnuts with 1/2 cup of the flour until the nuts are very finely ground. Transfer to a large bowl and stir in the sugar and remaining 1 cup flour. Toss in the butter until well coated, then press the butter into the dry ingredients with your fingertips to form pea-size clumps. Add the salted water and bring together with your hands until a shaggy dough forms.

3 Divide the dough into 2 disks, wrap tightly in plastic wrap, and refrigerate until firm, about 1 hour or up to overnight.

4 Preheat the oven to 375°F. Line several baking sheets with parchment paper.

5 Roll the dough between sheets of parchment paper until 1/8-inch thick. Use a lightly floured 4-inch fluted round cookie cutter, or another cookie cutter of your choice, to cut out as many rounds as possible. Gather and reroll the scraps to cut more rounds. You should have 20 cookies total. Transfer to the prepared pans, spacing them 1 inch apart. If the dough has softened, refrigerate again until firm.

6 In a small bowl, beat the egg white with the remaining 1 teaspoon water. Brush the egg wash over the dough, then sprinkle with sugar. Bake until golden brown, about 15 minutes. Cool completely on the sheets on wire racks.

· ·

Carla's Tips

• If you're feeling lazy, you can pulse the sugar and remaining flour into the walnut mixture in the food processor. You can then pulse in the butter until pea-size clumps form, then pulse in the water until a shaggy dough forms. I'm a fan of finishing the dough by hand, but it still works if you do it all in the machine.

· ·

Tea Cookies

I'll take tea anytime. It's not just because I don't drink alcohol or coffee; it's because I find the aromas and flavors of the hundreds of varieties out there fascinating and delicious. In the following cookie recipes, I treat tea as a seasoning, a concept I've been wanting to play with for years. It goes without saying that these cookies are meant to be enjoyed with a good leisurely cuppa tea in the company of friends and family.

INDIAN

Chocolate Chai Sandwich Cookies

Makes about 2 dozen

When life gets too crazy, I find few things more comforting than going to my local tea shop in D.C., SiTea, and sitting down to a steaming cup of chai. The spices put me at ease and I feel all's right with the world again. I wanted to capture that feeling in a cookie and figured chai with shortbread and chocolate would make me feel even better. It does.

2 cups all-purpose flour, plus more for rolling

¹/₂ teaspoon ground cinnamon

¹/₂ teaspoon table salt

¹/₂ pound (2 sticks) unsalted butter, at room temperature

¹/₂ cup sugar

1¹/₂ teaspoons vanilla extract

¹/₄ cup heavy cream

¹/₂ teaspoon loose-leaf chocolate chai or regular chai tea

¹/₄ cup finely chopped bittersweet or semisweet chocolate

1 In a small bowl, whisk the flour, cinnamon, and salt until well mixed.

2 In the bowl of an electric mixer fitted with the paddle, beat the butter and sugar on medium-high speed until creamy but still gritty, about 2 minutes. Beat in the vanilla extract. Reduce the speed to low and beat in the flour mixture just until the dough sticks together.

3 Form the dough into 2 disks, wrap tightly in plastic wrap, and refrigerate until firm, about 1 hour or up to overnight.

4 Preheat the oven to 325°F. Line several baking sheets with parchment paper.

5 Roll the dough between sheets of lightly floured parchment paper until ¼ inch thick. Use a lightly floured 2-inch round cookie cutter, or another cookie cutter of your choice, to cut out as many rounds as possible. Gather and reroll the scraps to cut more rounds. Transfer to the baking sheets, spacing them 1 inch apart. If the dough has softened, refrigerate again until firm.

6 Bake the rounds until pale golden (not brown), about 15 minutes.

7 While the cookies are baking, prepare the chai ganache: In a small pot, bring the cream just to a boil. Add the chai and reduce the heat to low. Steep for 5 minutes. Then place the chocolate in a medium bowl and strain the warm cream over it. Stir until smooth. Let the ganache cool until it is thick enough to spread, stirring it occasionally.

8 When the cookies are pale golden, remove them from the oven and let them cool on the pans on wire racks for 2 minutes. Then transfer the cookies to the wire racks and let cool completely.

9 Line the cooled cookies up in pairs, bottom sides up. Spoon ½ teaspoon of the chocolate chai ganache on one cookie of each pair. Sandwich with the tops and squeeze gently, being careful to not break the cookies. Let stand until the ganache firms up completely, about 30 minutes.

 ALL-AMERICAN

Lemon Citrus Tea Cookies

Makes about 3 dozen

Lemon's my go-to for savory and sweet. Instead of making cookies with the usual zest and juice, I thought it'd be fun to play with lemon in other forms, namely tea and extract. The key for these buttery rounds is to purchase all-natural ingredients that have true lemon flavors.

2 cups all-purpose flour, plus more for rolling

4 teaspoons high-quality loose-leaf herbal lemon tea, finely ground

1/2 teaspoon table salt

1/2 pound (2 sticks) unsalted butter, at room temperature

1/2 cup sugar

1 teaspoon lemon extract

1/2 teaspoon vanilla extract

1 In a small bowl, whisk the flour, loose-leaf tea, and salt until well mixed.

2 In the bowl of an electric mixer fitted with the paddle, beat the butter and sugar on medium-high speed until creamy but still gritty, about 2 minutes. Beat in the lemon and vanilla extracts. Reduce the speed to low and beat in the flour mixture just until the dough sticks together.

3 Form the dough into 2 disks, wrap tightly in plastic wrap, and refrigerate until firm, at least 1 hour or up to overnight.

4 Preheat the oven to 325°F. Line several baking sheets with parchment paper.

5 Roll the dough between sheets of lightly floured parchment paper until 1/4 inch thick. Use a lightly floured 2-inch round cookie cutter, or another cookie cutter of your choice, to cut out as many rounds as possible. Gather and reroll the scraps to cut more rounds. Transfer to the baking sheets, spacing them 1 inch apart. If the dough has softened, refrigerate again until firm.

6 Bake the rounds until pale golden (not brown), about 15 minutes. Cool on the pans on wire racks for 2 minutes. Then transfer the cookies to the wire racks and let cool completely.

Chocolate Mint Crinkle Cookies

Makes about 30 dozen

When I first created these cookies, it was Christmas in New York City and the deep mint-chocolate scent got me in the spirit of the season. In tea form, the mint flavor is subtler than extract (and candy canes!), so these pretty powdery chewies have a distinctly grown-up taste.

1 tablespoon premium loose-leaf mint tea leaves

1 cup granulated sugar

1 1/2 cups all-purpose flour

1 1/2 teaspoons baking powder

1/2 teaspoon table salt

1/4 cup unsweetened cocoa powder

8 tablespoons (1 stick) unsalted butter, melted

1/4 cup hot water

2 large eggs, beaten

1/2 cup mini dark chocolate chips

1 cup confectioner's sugar

1 In a spice grinder or blender, pulse the tea leaves and 1/4 cup of the granulated sugar until very finely ground. Transfer to a medium bowl and whisk in the flour, baking powder, salt, and remaining 3/4 cup granulated sugar.

2 In a large bowl, stir the cocoa powder, butter, and hot water until smooth. Stir in the eggs, and then gradually stir in the flour mixture. Fold in the chocolate chips. Cover and refrigerate until very firm, at least 6 hours and up to 1 day.

3 Preheat the oven to 375°F. Line several baking sheets with parchment paper. Put the confectioner's sugar in a shallow bowl.

4 Working in batches, form the dough into 1/2-inch balls. The best way to handle the sticky dough is to scoop up a level 1/2 teaspoon of dough, then use the tip of a butter knife to scoop it out of the spoon into the confectioner's sugar. Once coated, they can be gently shaped into perfect balls. Transfer the cookies to the baking sheets, spacing them 1 inch apart.

5 Bake until the cookies are cracked but still soft in the middle if pressed lightly, about 6 minutes. Cool completely on the pans on wire racks.

. . . .

Carla's Tips

• These are tiny bites: You form the dough into chickpea-size balls and they spread to the size of quarters. I really think they taste best this way, but you can make them bigger if you must.

• If you prefer fudgy cookies, bake these for 5 minutes. If you want them crisper, go longer. I find they hit that crisp-edge, chewy-center balance at 6 minutes, but your oven may be a bit different.

• **Swap Out:** Earl Grey is also amazing here, for a floral chocolate flavor.

. . . .

Corn Desserts

Corn's the star in sweets in other parts of the world. In America, we tend to treat corn as an ingredient for savory dishes or to use it in a sweet cornbread or breakfast muffin. But it makes sense for dessert because at its best, corn is super sweet and just starchy enough to taste like a treat.

 ALL-AMERICAN

Blueberry Corn Waffles

Makes about 6 Belgian waffles

Because corn has an earthy natural sweetness, I decided to throw it into waffles, which are great for breakfast and dessert. I love the tender, almost sugary, crunch of just-cut-off-the-cob kernels. Embedded in a crisp cornmeal waffle with bursting blueberries? Mmmmm, *that's heaven. You really should eat these right when they come out of the waffle iron because that's when their delicate crisp crust is crustiest and the inside is tender and moist and airy. I like to set up my waffle iron right on the kitchen table, with the batter on one side and a stack of plates on the other. Just dish 'em out as they're done and save at least one for yourself.*

1 cup all-purpose flour

1 cup fine stone-ground yellow cornmeal

1/3 cup sugar

1 1/2 tablespoons baking powder

1 teaspoon table salt

1 1/2 cups whole milk

4 large eggs, separated, at room temperature

1 cup fresh corn kernels, chopped

1/2 cup blueberries

8 tablespoons (1 stick) unsalted butter, melted

1 Heat a waffle iron to medium. Into a large bowl, sift together the flour, cornmeal, sugar, baking powder, and salt.

2 In a medium bowl, whisk the milk and egg yolks. Stir in the corn and blueberries, and then pour the liquid mixture into the flour mixture. Stir with a spatula until just combined, and then stir in the melted butter. The batter will be a little lumpy.

3 In a clean large bowl, beat the egg whites until soft peaks form. Gently fold half of the whites into the batter, then fold in the remaining whites until just incorporated.

4 Lightly grease your waffle iron if needed. Ladle a spoonful of batter into the waffle iron, close the iron, and cook until the waffle is golden brown, crisp, and cooked through. Different-size irons take different amounts of batter and cook differently; check your manufacturer's instructions for details. Eat right away!

• •

Carla's Tips

• It may seem like a hassle to whip egg whites, but they're the key to keeping these waffles light and airy inside.

• **Sweet Tooth:** Douse these with maple syrup or honey, and top with sweetened whipped cream or ice cream. I usually skip the whipped cream and slather butter on the hot waffles before pourin' on the syrup.

• •

 BRAZILIAN

Pure Corn Pudding

Serves 4

Sometimes, I see a recipe and I just have to try it because it sounds so fascinating. In this case, I couldn't imagine corn having enough starch to turn milk into pudding, but it does. At the height of summer, this is the ideal corn dessert because it lets the corn shine and it tastes as good cold as it does warm.

4 cups fresh corn kernels

3 cups whole milk

1/2 cup sugar

1/4 teaspoon ground cinnamon

1/4 teaspoon kosher salt

2 tablespoons unsalted butter, melted

1 In a blender, puree the corn, milk, sugar, cinnamon, and salt until smooth. Strain through a fine-mesh sieve into a large saucepan, pressing on the solids to extract as much liquid as possible. Discard the solids.

2 Heat the corn milk over high heat until bubbles begin to form around the edge of the pan. Reduce the heat and simmer, stirring frequently, until thickened, about 15 minutes. Stir in the butter. Serve warm, room temperature, or chilled.

● ●

Carla's Tips

• The cooler the pudding, the thicker it gets. If you prefer a thinner version, enjoy it warm. The chilled pudding is firm, and room temp is, for some, just right.

• **Sweet Tooth:** Stir in more sugar, to taste, at the end.

● ●

Sharin' the Love

The day I made this cake was the same day my bathroom fell apart. I'd been putting off work on it for years, hoping the plumbing and tile problems would magically disappear. Guess what? Plumbing problems don't go away by themselves. On a hot summer day, the toilet decided to totally break down and it looked like the rest of the bathroom was going to go with it. I hit speed-dial for my handyman.

Robert is the go-to guy for every house on my block in D.C. We've been calling him for over a decade and he always shows up with a smile and fixes whatever's ailin' us. When he checked out my bathroom, he gave a low, sad whistle and showed me how bad the situation was. He promised to get right on it and was back within half an hour with his sidekick, tools, and supplies.

I was so grateful, I wanted to give him and his assistant something I knew they'd appreciate. By late afternoon, they were tearin' apart my wrecked room and I was pulling my Quince Corn Cake out of the oven. I cut them big slices and got them to take a break to enjoy it. You should've seen the looks on their faces! You'd think I'd given them, well, a hunk of warm cake.

They loved that cake so much, they kept talking about it the next time they were back. I brought them other dishes to try, but it was the cake that really stuck with them. They told me it was a taste of their hometowns, and that's when I realized that baking with love is powerful enough to bring folks back home, no matter how far they've come.

SPANISH

Quince Corn Cake

Serves 12

"What?" you ask. "I've never heard of a traditional Spanish corn cake." Well, that's because it doesn't really exist. I kept seeing recipes for a Brazilian corn cake with guava paste. I was excited about trying the guava corn cake, but when I got to the store, I couldn't find guava anything anywhere. What I did see in the cheese section, though, were pretty packages of membrillo. A solid jelly-like paste made of quince, it's similar in taste and texture to guava paste. You've probably seen it on a cheese plate somewhere. I think it's nice scattered throughout this easy-peasy cake.

Unsalted butter, for the pan

1 cup fine stone-ground yellow cornmeal

1 cup all-purpose flour

1 cup sugar

1 teaspoon kosher salt

1 cup whole milk

1 cup canola oil

1 large egg

1/2 cup diced membrillo paste, plus more for garnish

1 Preheat the oven to 350°F. Butter the sides and bottom of a 9-inch springform pan, line the bottom with parchment paper, and then butter the sides and bottom again.

2 In a large bowl, whisk the cornmeal, flour, sugar, and salt. In another bowl, whisk the milk, oil, and egg until well blended. Whisk the wet into the dry ingredients until fully incorporated. Stir in the membrillo, and pour into the springform pan.

3 Bake until a toothpick inserted in the center comes out clean, about 40 minutes. Cool in the pan on a wire rack for 10 minutes. Then remove the sides and slide the cake off the bottom onto the rack; let it cool completely. Garnish with membrillo and serve.

. . . .

Carla's Tips

• If the membrillo sticks to your knife when you try to cut it, oil the blade.

• You may think, as I did, that this cake would look pretty if you serve it bottom side up so you can see the membrillo. But it doesn't. It's much nicer with the crusty top on top.

• **Sweet Tooth:** Top slices of cake with a scoop of ice cream.

. . . .

Coconut Tapioca Pudding

Serves 8

My husband, Matthew, a tapioca pudding connoisseur, assures me this is the best he's ever tasted. I've always been more of a rice pudding girl, but I'm really happy with this dessert. It's not globby or too sweet, and the crunch of the corn's a happy accent.

3¼ cups water

½ teaspoon kosher salt, plus more to taste

¼ cup small pearl tapioca

2 cups fresh corn kernels

2 tablespoons sugar, plus more to taste

1 teaspoon vanilla extract

¾ cup coconut milk

1 In a medium saucepan, bring the water and salt to a boil. Stir in the tapioca and boil gently, stirring occasionally, until just tender, about 5 minutes. The tiny pearls will be chewy on the outside and a little firm on the inside. They should be almost clear, with a central white spot.

2 Stir in the corn, sugar, and vanilla. Heat to a simmer, and then stir in the coconut milk. Continue simmering until the tapioca is just translucent and the corn crisp-tender, about 7 minutes. Season to taste with more salt and sugar. Serve warm, room temperature, or chilled. It becomes firm as it cools.

• •

Carla's Tips

• Tapioca reminds me of the eye of the tiger. As it simmers, the outside becomes translucent before the center does, so you end up with a pot of eyes looking up at you. Okay, that sounds unappetizing, but tapioca pearls are totally fascinating in the way they cook. You don't want to overcook them or you'll end up with mushy pudding. Take them off the heat as soon as the little dots in the centers disappear.

• **Sweet Tooth:** Stir in more sugar, to taste, at the end. The amount you add will depend on how sweet your corn is.

• •

Acknowledgments

I have had the pleasure of talking with, observing, questioning, and dining with many people over the years and around the world, and they are all a part of this book—which is as much about relationships as it is about food. Many thanks to all those folks.

More specifically, I'd like to thank those who are directly related to the existence of my second cookbook:

My husband, Matthew, who continues to be a pillar of strength for me. Thanks for your patience during recipe testing, tasting, and my constant chatter about what was going on and where I was in the process. My stepson, Noah, for being willing to try anything at least once.

My mom, Audrey Hall, who continues to be my biggest cheerleader and supporter, as well as my sister, Kim, her husband, Gus, and my niece and nephews. Thanks for always keeping it "real" and being my inspiration for helping folks get back into the kitchen.

Genevieve Ko, my co-author, recipe tester, friend, and metronome, for making this daunting task more fun than I ever thought possible. I thoroughly enjoyed the many weeks of research, recipe testing, and eating! Thanks to Dave and the girls for always making room for me at your dinner table when the testing ran late.

Janis Donnaud, my literary agent, for her strength and belief in me. Thanks for being in my corner and a force to be reckoned with.

My editor, Leslie Meredith, of Atria Books, for her excitement and genuine interest in food and food culture. I'm grateful for the Atria Books team's new and fresh perspective. Thanks to president and publisher Judith Curr, associate publisher Benjamin Lee, senior jacket art director Jeanne Lee, assistant director of publicity Lisa Sciambra, publishing manager Jackie Jou, and associate editor Donna Loffredo.

My beauty team, affectionately called The J-Squad—Jaclyn Hunt, Jeanna Mirante, and Jill McKay—for making me look and feel pretty every day on *The Chew* and now in my second cookbook.

To Jennifer Barry, book designer, thank you for bringing the recipes and photographs alive with your vision of color, texture, and layout. I love it! And many thanks to the photo team: photographer Frances Janisch, digital tech Jody Kivort, food stylist Michael Pederson, and prop stylists and assistants Kira Corbin and Jenna Tedesco.

A huge thanks to everyone out there who has taught me about food and the love that comes along with it.

— Carla Hall

Thank you first and foremost to Carla, for being a great chef and friend. Each and every cooking (and tasting!) session was so much fun because of your infectious love of amazing flavor. Your enthusiasm, kindness, and generosity of spirit are unparalleled.

I'm grateful to Matthew and Noah for letting me invade their home and steal Carla for this book. You guys are so welcoming!

Thanks to Atria's and Jennifer Barry's teams for putting this book together and to my agent, Angela Miller, and to Janis Donnaud, for making it possible.

Last, but not least, thanks to my family and Izzy for being so supportive.

— Genevieve Ko

Index

About the Authors

Carla Hall is a co-host of ABC Daytime's lifestyle series *The Chew,* seated alongside restaurateurs and *Iron Chef America* stars Mario Batali and Michael Symon, entertaining expert Clinton Kelly, and health and wellness enthusiast Daphne Oz. Carla is also well known as a past competitor and fan favorite on Bravo's *Top Chef.* Carla is the owner of Carla Hall Petite Cookies, an artisan cookie company that specializes in creating sweet and savory "petite bites of love." Her approach to cooking blends her classic French training and her Southern upbringing for a twist on traditional favorites. Carla is committed to health and balance in everyday living.

A native of Nashville, Tennessee, Carla received a degree in accounting from Howard University, but traveling through Europe awakened her passion for food and inspired a new career path. Carla attended L'Academie de Cuisine in Maryland, where she completed her culinary training, and then went on to work as a sous chef at the Henley Park Hotel in Washington, D.C. She also served as executive chef at both The State Plaza Hotel and The Washington Club and has taught classes at CulinAerie and her alma mater, L'Academie de Cuisine. Carla lives in Washington, D.C., with her husband, Matthew Lyons, and stepson, Noah.

Genevieve Ko is a food writer who has worked with renowned chef Jean-Georges Vongerichten on *The Asian Flavors of Jean-Georges* and *Home Cooking with Jean-Georges* and with pastry chef Pichet Ong on *The Sweet Spot: Asian-Inspired Desserts.* She also has developed recipes for, written, and edited a number of other cookbooks. Previously an editor at *Gourmet* and *Good Housekeeping*, Genevieve is currently contributing food editor at *Health*, where she creates recipes and writes food stories.